SARASOTA UNCOVERED

Your Ultimate Guide to Florida's Gem

Travel Like a Local
Florida's Coastal Utopia

Dive into Sarasota, Florida's most genuine experiences and hidden treasures, with this local guide.

Word Wave Publishing
wordwavepublishing.com

SARASOTA UNCOVERED

Mike Avey

SARASOTA UNCOVERED

Copyright © 2023 by Word Wave Publishing

All rights reserved. No part of this publication may be reproduced, distributed, or transmitted in any form or by any means, including photocopying, recording, or other electronic or mechanical methods, without the prior written permission of the publisher, except in the case of brief quotations embodied in critical reviews and specific other noncommercial uses permitted by copyright law.

First Edition, 2023

ISBN: 9798393040789

Published by Word Wave Publishing

Youngstown, OH 12345

www.wordwavepublishing.com

info@wordwavepublishing.com

The information in this book we diligently researched and is accurate as of the time of publication. However, the author and publisher refuse responsibility for errors, omissions, or changes in details such as addresses, phone numbers, or websites. Readers are advised to verify the information before relying independently upon it. Neither Mike Avey nor Word Wave Publishing is sponsored by, affiliated with, or acting as an agent for any vendors or companies mentioned in this book.

TABLE CONTENTS

Chapter 1 / Adventure Sports _____ *5*

Chapter 2 / Amusement Parks _____ *10*

Chapter 3 / Beaches _____ *15*

Chapter 4 / Cycling _____ *22*

Chapter 5 / Eco-Tourism _____ *27*

Chapter 6 / Fishing _____ *34*

Chapter 7 / Geocaching _____ *41*

Chapter 8 / Golfing _____ *45*

Chapter 9 /. Hiking Nature Walks _____ *51*

Chapter 10 / Horseback Riding _____ *57*

Chapter 11 / Kayaking Paddle Board _____ *62*

Chapter 12 / Family Fun with Kids _____ *67*

Chapter 13 / Wildlife and Bird Watching _____ *73*

Chapter 14 / Casino Gambling _____ *79*

Chapter 15 / City tours _____ *82*

Chapter 16 / Historical Sites _____ *86*

Chapter 17 / Movie Theater _____ *90*

Chapter 18 / Museums _____ *94*

Chapter 19 / Spa, Yoga, Meditation _____ *100*

Chapter 20 / Theater Performances _____ *104*

Chapter 21 / Malls and Shopping _____ *107*

SARASOTA UNCOVERED

Chapter 22 / Farmer Markets _____ 109

Chapter 23 / Art Galleries _____ 113

Chapter 24 / Independent coffee cafes _____ 117

Chapter 25 / Restaurants _____ 122

Chapter 26 / Quick Eating _____ 129

Chapter 27 / Bars and Nightclubs _____ 134

Chapter 28 / Wine and Liquor Stores _____ 139

Chapter 29 /. CRAFT BREWERIES _____ 142

Chapter 30 / A Spirited Journey _____ 147

Chapter 31 / Uncorking the Magic _____ 151

Chapter 32 / Places to Stay _____ 155

Chapter 33 / Camping _____ 163

Chapter 34 / Airport Transportation: _____ 168

Chapter 35 / Weather _____ 172

: Chapter 36 / Traveler Resource _____ 174

Chapter 37 / Emergency Numbers Hospitals and Walk-In Clinics
_____ 176

ABOUT THE AUTHOR _____ 179

MIKE AVEY

Introduction

Welcome to Sarasota, Florida - the Sunshine State's hidden gem nestled along the sparkling Gulf Coast! This delightful coastal city boasts a rich tapestry of arts, culture, and natural beauty that will have you falling in love at first sight. This book will take you on a sun-kissed journey through Sarasota's intriguing history, iconic landmarks, unique attractions, and breathtaking surroundings. So, please sit back, relax, and let your imagination run wild as we explore this vibrant slice of paradise.

Overview of the City

Sarasota, affectionately known as "Florida's Cultural Coast," is a medium-sized city on the southwestern coast of Florida. With just under 60,000, this charming city is steeped in history and culture, offering visitors a laid-back vibe that is hard to resist. Sarasota's roots date back to the early 20th century. When it was a hub for the arts, attracting the likes of circus magnate John Ringling, who left an indelible mark on the city's landscape.

The city's picturesque coastline has pristine white-sand beaches, lush nature reserves, and swaying palm trees. At the same time, the downtown area boasts stunning architectural gems that reflect Sarasota's diverse history. The iconic landmarks include the Ringling Museum of Art, the Ca' d'Zan Mansion, and the whimsical Sarasota Opera House.

Sarasota's thriving economy is primarily driven by tourism, healthcare, and education, with a growing focus on technology and innovation. Visitors will find a bustling city that effortlessly balances a lively arts scene with a relaxed coastal lifestyle.

Unique Features and Attractions

Sarasota is a treasure trove of unique experiences that set it apart from other cities. Culture vultures will be delighted by the city's numerous art galleries, theaters, and museums, including the Ringling Museum of Art, which houses an impressive collection of European masterpieces, and the Mote Marine Laboratory & Aquarium, where visitors can learn about the diverse marine life of the Gulf Coast.

If you love nature, enjoy the Marie Selby Botanical Gardens, a tropical oasis highlighting rare and beautiful plants

SARASOTA UNCOVERED

worldwide. To taste Old Florida's charm, visit the Historic Spanish Point, a 30-acre archaeological and historical site that tells the story of Sarasota's early inhabitants.

Foodies will rejoice in Sarasota's eclectic culinary scene, which offers everything from fresh seafood to vibrant ethnic cuisine. Be sure to try some locally caught grouper or stone crab and remember to sample the city's famous Amish-made pies for dessert!

Surrounding Area

Sarasota's stunning natural beauty extends beyond the city limits, making it an ideal destination for outdoor enthusiasts. Just a short drive away, you will find the idyllic barrier islands of Siesta Key, Longboat Key, and Lido Key, where you can soak up the sun, stroll along the powdery white sand, or indulge in world-class fishing.

For a more adventurous escape, head to Myakka River State Park, one of Florida's oldest and largest parks, which offers miles of hiking and biking trails, canoeing, and wildlife-watching opportunities. And if you are a golf lover, you will be pleased to know that the Sarasota area is home to over 50 top-rated golf courses, each with unique challenges and picturesque views.

In short, Sarasota is a captivating coastal city that promises an unforgettable experience for visitors. From its rich cultural heritage and awe-inspiring natural beauty to its unique attractions and mouth-watering cuisine, there is something for everyone to enjoy. So, what are you waiting for? Pack your bags, grab your sunscreen, and discover the magic of Sarasota, Florida, for yourself!

We hope this introduction to Sarasota has piqued your interest and inspired you to embark on your Floridian adventure. As you explore this enchanting city and its surrounding areas, we are confident you will fall under its spell like countless others before you. So, grab your shades and flip-flops, and get ready to experience Sarasota, Florida's warmth, wonder, and charm - a place where memories are just waiting to be made.

Chapter 1 /
Adventure Sports

Adventure sports are thrilling, adrenaline-pumping activities that push the boundaries of physical and mental endurance, often taking place in breathtaking natural environments. These exhilarating pursuits challenge participants to step outside their comfort zones, testing their limits while offering unforgettable experiences.

Encompass various disciplines, each designed to awaken the senses and inspire awe. Some famous examples, biking, skydiving, water sports, and surfing, to name a few.

One of the critical aspects of adventure sports is the element of risk, which can heighten the sense of excitement and accomplishment. Participants often confront their fears, learn valuable life skills, and forge lasting bonds with adventurers.

Safety is always a top priority, with proper training, equipment, and guidance ensuring that risks are minimized while the thrill of the experience remains intact.

The allure of adventure sports lies in their adrenaline rush and the opportunity to connect with nature, explore new landscapes, and immerse oneself in the beauty of the great outdoors. As participants push their physical limits and conquer personal challenges, they often develop a deeper appreciation for the world around them.

In conclusion, adventure sports offer a unique blend of excitement, challenge, and personal growth that can be both exhilarating and transformative. For thrill-seekers and nature enthusiasts, these activities provide the perfect opportunity to forge unforgettable memories while testing one's mettle in some of the world's most stunning settings.

Each adventure sport offers a unique and thrilling way to experience Sarasota's natural beauty and excitement and the greater Southwest Florida area.

Jet Skiing:
CB's Saltwater Outfitters
Phone: (941) 349-4400   www.cbsoutfitters.com/

CB's Saltwater Outfitters offers jet ski rentals for a thrilling adventure on the water. Enjoy an exciting ride along the beautiful coastline of Siesta Key with well-maintained equipment and safety guidelines in place.

SARASOTA UNCOVERED

Parasailing:
Siesta Key Watersports
Phone: (941) 921-3030
www.siestakeywatersports.com

Siesta Key Watersports offers unforgettable parasailing experiences, soaring high above the Gulf of Mexico. Choose from different heights and enjoy a bird's-eye view of the stunning coastline, clear waters, and marine life below.

Kiteboarding:
Sarasota Kiteboarding Le ssons & Tours
(941) 447-8010:
www.sarasotakiteboardinglessons.com

Learn to kiteboard with Sarasota Kiteboarding Lessons & Tours, which offers personalized lessons for all skill levels. Their experienced instructors will guide you through the basics and advanced techniques, ensuring a safe and exhilarating experience on the water.

Scuba Diving and Snorkeling:
Florida Underwater Sports
Phone: (941) 870-4461
www.floridaunderwatersports.com/

Florida Underwater Sports offers scuba diving, snorkeling trips, and certification courses. Explore the wonders of the Gulf of Mexico, including vibrant coral reefs, shipwrecks, and diverse marine life, with their knowledgeable and friendly staff.
Ziplining:

Blue Water Explorers
Phone: (941) 870-2494
www.bluewaterexplorers.com/

Blue Water Explorers offers scuba diving and snorkeling trips around Sarasota and the surrounding areas. They specialize in guided dives to shipwrecks, ledges, and reefs, allowing you to explore the underwater world and encounter various.

Marine Species.
Silent World Dive Center
Phone: (941) 359-9700
www.silentworlddivecenter.com

Silent World Dive Center is a full-service dive shop that offers scuba diving, snorkeling trips, and PADI certification courses. Their experienced staff will ensure a safe and enjoyable underwater adventure, whether you are a beginner or an experienced diver.

Dive Florida - Scuba & Snorkeling Adventures
Phone: (941) 755-3483
www.diveflorida.com/

Dive Florida offers a range of scuba diving and snorkeling adventures, including trips to reefs, wrecks, and other underwater sites. They cater to divers of all skill levels and provide personalized service to make your diving experience memorable and fun.

Adventure Diving Crystal River
Phone: (352) 795-7033
www.adventuredivecenter.net/

Adventure Diving Crystal River, although a bit further north from Sarasota, offers scuba diving and snorkeling trips in the Crystal River area. They are well-known for their manatee snorkeling tours, giving you a unique opportunity to interact with these gentle giants in their natural habitat.

SARASOTA UNCOVERED

TreeUmph! Adventure Course
www.treeumph.com/

TreeUmph! Adventure Course provides an exhilarating ziplining experience and other aerial challenges like obstacle courses and suspension bridges. Navigate through treetops and conquer your fears in a safe, fun, and adrenaline-pumping environment.

Wildlife Tours:
Around the Bend Nature Tours
Phone: (941) 794-8773
www.aroundbend.com/

Around the Bend Nature Tours specializes in guided eco-tours highlighting the region's diverse wildlife and ecosystems. Their knowledgeable guides will take you on boat tours, airboat rides, or walking tours, offering an immersive experience of Southwest Florida's natural habitats.

Each of these vendors offers a unique and exciting way to explore and enjoy the adventure sports in the Sarasota and Southwest Florida area.

Chapter 2 /
Amusement Parks

Florida is renowned for its fantastic array of amusement and theme parks, attracting millions of visitors annually. The Sunshine State boasts a diverse collection of exhilarating attractions that provide unforgettable experiences, ranging from adrenaline-pumping and captivating live performances to interactive exhibits and breathtaking-themed environments. Within a mere 3-hour radius of Sarasota, you'll find a variety of theme parks that cater to families, thrill-seekers, and everyone in between, offering a myriad of adventures and memories waiting to be created.

As you embark on a journey to explore the magical world of theme parks around Sarasota, you'll be delighted by the many options available. Discover the enchanting world of Walt Disney World Resort in Orlando, where dreams come to life through the Magic Kingdom, Epcot, Disney's Hollywood

SARASOTA UNCOVERED

Studios, and Disney's Animal Kingdom. Be captivated by the mesmerizing combination of wildlife conservation and thrilling rides at Busch Gardens Tampa Bay, where African-inspired adventures are just around the corner. Experience the magic of movies at Universal Orlando Resort, where you can immerse yourself in the Wizarding World of Harry Potter or join your favorite superheroes in epic battles at Universal's Islands of Adventure.

In addition to these well-known theme park giants, hidden gems scattered across the region offer unique experiences for every taste. Take a step back at the enchanting LEGOLAND Florida Resort, where childhood fantasies come to life through intricate LEGO creations and interactive play areas. Dive into the marine world at SeaWorld Orlando and encounter fascinating marine creatures while experiencing awe-inspiring roller coasters and aquatic shows. Feel the need for speed at Fun Spot America, where go-kart racing and classic amusement park rides create lasting memories for the whole family.

The vast cultural landscape of amusement parks within 3 hours of Sarasota offers something for everyone, ensuring a thrilling and unforgettable experience for all who venture into this exciting realm. Whether you're a roller coaster enthusiast, a theme park lover, or simply looking for a fun-filled day with the family, the amusement parks around Sarasota will exceed your expectations and leave you longing for more. So buckle up, hold on tight, and get ready to embark on a whirlwind adventure through the exciting world of Florida's theme parks!

Busch Gardens Tampa Bay
(1 hour, 5 minutes from Sarasota)
10165 N McKinley Dr, Tampa, FL 33612

Busch Gardens Tampa Bay combines exhilarating thrill rides, captivating live shows, and up-close animal encounters in a sprawling African-themed park. With adrenaline-pumping roller coasters, like Tigris and SheiKra, and a wide variety of family-friendly attractions, there is something for everyone to enjoy.

Adventure Island
(1 hour, 5 minutes from Sarasota)
10001 N McKinley Dr, Tampa, FL 33612

Adjacent to Busch Gardens Tampa Bay, Adventure Island is a 30-acre water park with various water slides, wave pools, and lazy rivers. It is an ideal place to cool off and enjoy water-based fun with the entire family.

LEGOLAND Florida Resort
(1 hour, 30 minutes from Sarasota)
1 Legoland Way, Winter Haven, FL 33884

This 150-acre, LEGO-themed park caters to families with children aged 2-12. It features more than 50 rides, shows, and attractions, including a water park and a botanical garden. LEGOLAND Florida Resort brings the world of LEGO to life with themed lands, interactive exhibits, and life-sized LEGO models.

Walt Disney World Resort
(2 hours from Sarasota)
Walt Disney World Resort, Orlando, FL 32830

The iconic Walt Disney World Resort in Orlando has four theme parks: Magic Kingdom, Epcot, Disney's Hollywood Studios, and Disney's Animal Kingdom. Each park offers a unique blend of attractions, entertainment, and dining experiences that celebrate the magic of Disney and cater to visitors of all ages.

SARASOTA UNCOVERED

Universal Orlando Resort
(2 hours, 10 minutes from Sarasota)
6000 Universal Blvd, Orlando, FL 32819

Universal Orlando Resort features two theme parks, Universal Studios Florida and Universal's Islands of Adventure, along with the Volcano Bay water park. The resort is known for its thrilling attractions based on popular movies and TV shows, such as Harry Potter, Jurassic Park, and Transformers, as well as its immersive themed lands like The Wizarding World of Harry Potter.

SeaWorld Orlando
(2 hours, 10 minutes from Sarasota)
7007 Sea World Dr, Orlando, FL 32821

SeaWorld Orlando offers unique marine life exhibits, educational experiences, and thrilling rides. Visitors can learn about the world's oceans and inhabitants while enjoying roller coasters like Mako and Kraken and engaging shows featuring dolphins, sea lions, and orcas.

Aquatica Orlando
(2 hours, 10 minutes from Sarasota)
5800 Water Play Way, Orlando, FL 32821

Aquatica Orlando is SeaWorld's water park, boasting thrilling water slides, wave pools, and lazy rivers. The park features unique attractions like the Dolphin Plunge, a slide that sends riders through a pool filled with dolphins, and Roa's Rapids, a fast-paced river adventure.

Fun Spot America
(2 hours, 15 minutes from Sarasota)
5700 Fun Spot Way, Orlando, FL 32819

Fun Spot America is a family-owned theme park that offers a more laid-back and affordable experience compared to the larger parks in the area. Entertaining Spot America is a great place for a fun day out with the family, with roller coasters, go-kart tracks, and an assortment of classic midway rides.

Gatorland
(2 hours, 20 minutes from Sarasota)
14501 S Orange Blossom Trl, Orlando, FL 32837

Gatorland is a unique wildlife attraction that focuses on alligators and crocodiles. The park features various exhibits, live shows, and hands-on encounters with these fascinating reptiles. Visitors can also enjoy the Scream in' Gator Zip Line, which takes them on an exhilarating ride above the park's alligator breeding marsh.

SARASOTA UNCOVERED

Chapter 3 / Beaches

Florida's sun-kissed beaches are a paradise for vacationers seeking relaxation, fun, and adventure. With miles of pristine coastline, warm waters, and a laid-back atmosphere, it is no wonder that millions of visitors flock to the Sunshine State each year. While basking in the sun and splashing in the surf can be a dream come true, it is essential to prioritize personal safety to ensure that your beach getaway remains a memorable and enjoyable experience.

Sun safety is necessary when you are spending time at the beach. The sun's rays can be intense in Florida, but that should not stop you from having a blast outdoors. Instead, apply a broad-spectrum sunscreen with an SPF of 30 or higher to protect your skin from harmful UVA and UVB rays. Do not forget to reapply every two hours or immediately after swimming, as water can wash away the sunscreen. Wearing a wide-brimmed hat, sunglasses with UV protection, and lightweight, long-sleeved clothing can also help shield your skin from the sun's rays.

Staying hydrated is another crucial aspect of sun safety. Make it a point to drink plenty of water throughout the day to replace the fluids lost through sweat. Avoid excessive consumption of alcohol, as it can lead to dehydration and impair your judgment, making water-related activities riskier.

Water safety should be a top priority when enjoying Florida's beautiful beaches. Continuously swim with a buddy and keep a close eye on children playing near the water. Pay attention to posted warning signs and flags, as they can provide essential information about water conditions, such as rip currents or dangerous marine life. Consider wearing a life jacket if you are not a strong swimmer or venturing deeper waters.

Remember that the ocean can be unpredictable, and rip currents pose a significant hazard to swimmers. If you are caught in a rip current, do not panic, or try to swim against it. Instead, stay calm and swim parallel to the shore until you are out of the current, then swim back to land at an angle.

Lastly, be mindful of your personal belongings while at the beach. Keep your valuables locked in your vehicle or hotel room and avoid leaving items unattended. It is also wise to familiarize yourself with the beach's layout and know the location of the nearest lifeguard station or emergency services in case of an accident.

Following these simple safety tips ensures your Florida beach vacation is filled with fun, relaxation, and unforgettable memories. So, grab your sunscreen, shades, and swimsuit, and get ready to soak up the sun on Florida's beautiful shores!

Siesta Key Beach:
948 Beach Rd, Sarasota, FL 34242, USA.

Known for its award-winning, powdery white quartz sand, Siesta Key Beach is a top-rated beach in the United States. The beach offers a relaxed atmosphere with clear waters, perfect for swimming, sunbathing, or playing beach volleyball. Visitors can enjoy spectacular sunsets, a large playground, and nearby shops and restaurants.

Lido Key Beach:
400 Benjamin Franklin Dr, Sarasota, FL 34236, USA.
A favorite among locals and tourists alike, Lido Key Beach offers a range of amenities, including restrooms, picnic areas, a playground, and ample parking. The beach's calm waters are great for swimming and paddleboarding, while the nearby St. Armands Circle provides shopping and dining options. 400 Benjamin Franklin Dr, Sarasota, FL 34236, USA.

Longboat Key:
Longboat Key, Florida, USA.
This beautiful barrier island boasts miles of pristine beaches, luxurious resorts, and excellent dining options. The island's tranquil atmosphere makes it perfect for those seeking a more relaxed vacation experience, with opportunities for golfing, tennis, and spa treatments.

Turtle Beach:
8918 Midnight Pass Road, Sarasota, FL 34242, USA.
Situated on the southern end of Siesta Key, Turtle Beach is a more secluded option with fewer crowds and excellent shelling opportunities. The beach's amenities include restrooms, picnic areas, and a boat launch, making it ideal for families and nature lovers.

Nokomis Beach:
100 Casey Key Road, Nokomis, FL 34275, USA.
This family-friendly beach offers a laid-back atmosphere with amenities like picnic facilities, restrooms, and free parking. The beach is known for shark tooth hunting, and the nearby North Jetty Park provides an excellent spot for fishing and watching boats pass by. 100 Casey Key Rd, Nokomis, FL 34275, USA.

SARASOTA UNCOVERED

Venice Beach:
101 The Esplanade S, Venice, FL 34285, USA.
As the "Shark Tooth Capital of the World," Venice Beach is famous for its fossilized shark teeth finds. The beach offers a picturesque setting for sunbathing, swimming, snorkeling, a fishing pier, and a pavilion with restrooms and concessions.

Caspersen Beach:
4100 Harbor Dr, Venice, FL 34285, USA.
This secluded and natural beach is perfect for those seeking a serene experience away from the crowds. The beach's undeveloped shoreline provides a prime spot for shelling, birdwatching, and enjoying a peaceful walk.

Anna Maria Island:
4100 Harbor Dr, Venice, FL 34285, USA.
Just a short drive from Sarasota, Anna Maria Island is a quaint island destination with stunning beaches, excellent dining options, and charming shops. The island's laid-back vibe, friendly locals, and beautiful sunsets make it a popular vacation choice.

Coquina Beach:
2650 Gulf Dr, Bradenton Beach, FL 34217, USA.
Located on the southern end of Anna Maria Island, Coquina Beach offers a family-friendly atmosphere with shaded picnic areas, playgrounds, and clear waters. The nearby Coquina Baywalk provides a scenic boardwalk through the mangroves, perfect for birdwatching and nature photography.

Manatee Public Beach:
4000 Gulf Dr, Holmes Beach, FL 34217, USA.
Manatee Public Beach is a famous beach on Anna Maria Island. It is known for its many amenities, including restrooms, picnic areas, and beachside dining options at the Anna Maria Island Cafe. The beach also features a playground, volleyball courts, and lifeguards on duty.

Bradenton Beach:
100 Gulf Dr, Bradenton Beach, FL 34217, USA.
Bradenton Beach is a charming destination on Anna Maria Island, featuring a historic pier, an inviting atmosphere, and beautiful sunsets. The beach's soft sand and calm waters make it an excellent choice for swimming and sunbathing, while nearby Bridge Street offers shops and restaurants.

Crescent Beach:
6490 Midnight Pass Rd, Sarasota, FL 34242, USA.
Located on Siesta Key, Crescent Beach is a quieter alternative to Siesta Key Beach, offering seclusion and a more peaceful experience. The beach's smooth sand and clear waters make it perfect for swimming, sunbathing, and beachcombing.

North Lido Beach:
400 John Ringling Blvd, Sarasota, FL 34236, USA.
Situated on Lido Key, North Lido Beach is less crowded, featuring natural dunes and a more private setting. The beach is ideal for those seeking a peaceful getaway with sunbathing, swimming, and birdwatching opportunities. In addition, St. Armands Circle offers shopping and dining options a short walk away.

South Lido Park:
2201 Benjamin Franklin Dr, Sarasota, FL 34236, USA.
This nature park combines beach relaxation with various recreational activities. South Lido Park offers access to the Gulf of Mexico and Sarasota Bay, with beaches, picnic areas, and trails for walking or jogging. Visitors can enjoy kayaking, paddle boarding, and birdwatching in the park's mangrove tunnels and estuaries.

SARASOTA UNCOVERED

Sarasota Bayfront Park:
1 Marina Plaza, Sarasota, FL 34236, USA.
A popular spot for waterfront relaxation, Sarasota Bayfront Park offers stunning views of the bay, marina, and downtown Sarasota. The park features walking paths, open green spaces, and a children's splash pad, making it a great place to unwind and enjoy the coastal scenery.

Ted Sperling Park:
190 Taft Dr, Sarasota, FL 34236, USA.
Located at the southern end of Lido Key, Ted Sperling Park offers access to Lido Key Beach and South Lido Park. The park features kayaks, paddleboard rentals, and nature trails that meander through the mangroves. Visitors can also spot local wildlife, including birds, dolphins, and manatees.

Palma Sola Causeway Park:
8599 Manatee Ave W, Bradenton, FL 34209, USA.
Positioned on the causeway to Anna Maria Island, Palma Sola Causeway Park provides beach access, picnic areas, and shallow waters perfect for wading. The park is a popular spot for windsurfing, kiteboarding, and paddleboarding, and it offers scenic views of the bay and surrounding mangroves.

Beer Can Island:
North Shore Rd, Longboat Key, FL 34228, USA.
A hidden gem on the north end of Longboat Key, Beer Can Island is known for its driftwood and secluded atmosphere. Accessible by boat or walking during low tide, this small beach offers a unique experience for those seeking a more adventurous and off-the-beaten-path destination.

Chapter 4 / Cycling

Sarasota is a haven for cycling enthusiasts, with its picturesque landscapes, stunning waterfronts, and quaint neighborhoods that beckon riders to explore. The region offers various on- and off-road cycling routes for cyclists of all skill levels. The area's warm climate and vibrant cycling community make Sarasota an attractive destination for those looking to include some pedal-powered adventure in their trip.

Here is a list of excellent on-road and off-road cycling locations in and around Sarasota, along with the best access points and a brief description of each trail or area:

SARASOTA UNCOVERED

Legacy Trail
Access: Culverhouse Park, 7301 McIntosh Rd, Sarasota, FL 34238
This 12.5-mile trail connects Sarasota to Venice, following a historic railroad corridor through natural habitats, parks, and urban areas.

Venetian Waterway Park
Caspersen Beach Park, 4100 Harbor Dr, Venice, FL 34285
This 9.3-mile trail runs alongside both banks of the Intracoastal Waterway, offering picturesque views and opportunities for wildlife spotting.

Myakka River State Park
Access Main entrance, 13208 State Rd 72, Sarasota, FL 34241
With over 39 miles of biking trails, this park provides diverse terrains, including paved roads, dirt trails, and boardwalks through wetlands.

The John and Mable Ringling Causeway
Bird Key Park, 200 John Ringling Blvd, Sarasota, FL 34236
This 3-mile round-trip ride offers panoramic views of the Sarasota skyline, marina, and Sarasota Bay as you cross the iconic Ringling Bridge.

Longboat Key
Access point: Quick Point Nature Reserve, 100 Gulf of Mexico Dr, Longboat Key, FL 34228
This 11-mile-long barrier island provides a scenic ride along the Gulf of Mexico with picturesque beach views and access to nature reserves.

Rothenbach Park
Access: Main entrance, 8650 Bee Ridge Rd, Sarasota, FL 34241
The park features a 2-mile paved loop with gentle hills, providing a family-friendly and accessible ride through a natural setting.

Oscar Scherer State Park
Access: Main entrance, 1843 S Tamiami Trail, Osprey, FL 34229
With over 15 miles of trails, this park offers paved and off-road cycling experiences through diverse habitats, including scrubby flatwoods and pine forests.

Celery Fields
Celery Fields parking, 6893 Palmer Blvd, Sarasota, FL 34240
This regional stormwater facility features a 1.5-mile paved loop and boardwalks through wetlands, offering wildlife spotting and birdwatching opportunities.

Sarasota Bayfront Park
Access point: Main entrance, 1 Marina Plaza, Sarasota, FL 34236
This waterfront park offers a scenic ride along the bay with views of the marina, downtown Sarasota, and the iconic Unconditional Surrender statue.

Carlton Reserve
Main entrance, 1800 Mabry Carlton Pkwy, Venice, FL 34292
With over 100 miles of trails, this natural area provides off-road cycling experiences through diverse habitats, including pine flatwoods, prairies, and wetlands.

SARASOTA UNCOVERED

Bike Rental and Service

For bicycle rentals in Sarasota, here is a list of businesses, along with their physical address, phone number, website address, and whether they offer electric bikes:

Endless Summer Eco Tours & Rentals
190 Taft Dr, Lido Key, Sarasota, FL 34236
Phone: (941) 376-0287: www.endlesssummerflorida.com/
Electric Bikes: Yes

Ryder Bikes
527 S Pineapple Ave, Sarasota, FL 34236
Phone: (941) 260-0333   www.ryderbikes.com/
Electric Bikes: Yes

Village Bikes
8111 Lakewood Main St, Bradenton, FL 34202
Phone: (941) 388-0550   www.villagebikes.com/
Electric Bikes: Yes

Pedego Sarasota
3894 Cattlemen Rd, Sarasota, FL 34233
Phone: (941) 993-2618
www.pedegoelectricbikes.com/dealers/sarasota/
Electric Bikes: Yes (specializes in electric bikes)

Siesta Key Bike & Kayak
1224 Old Stickney Point Rd, Sarasota, FL 34242
Phone:(941) 346-0891
www.siestakeybikeandkayak.com/
Electric Bikes: Yes

I Bike Sarasota
1525 4th St, Sarasota, FL 34236
Phone: (941) 376-3368   www.ibikesarasota.com/
Electric Bikes: Yes

Ride & Paddle by Siesta Sports Rentals
6551 Midnight Pass Rd, Sarasota, FL 34242
Phone: (941) 346-1797
www.siestasportsrentals.com/
Electric Bikes: Yes

Robinhood Rentals
5121 Ocean Blvd, Sarasota, FL 34242
Phone: (941) 554-4242   www.robinhoodrentals.com/
Electric Bikes: Yes

Sarasota Bike Tours
1700 Ken Thompson Pkwy, Sarasota, FL 34236
Phone: (941) 356-4386 www.sarasotabiketours.com/
Electric Bikes: No

ABC Bicycle & Jet Ski Rentals
1930 Stickney Point Rd, Sarasota, FL 34231
Phone: (941) 921-5342   www.abcbikesjetskis.com/
Electric Bikes: No

SARASOTA UNCOVERED

Chapter 5 / Eco-Tourism

Eco-tourism is a rapidly growing trend in the travel industry, focused on promoting sustainable and responsible practices that minimize negative impacts on the environment and support the well-being of local communities. At its core, eco-tourism seeks to foster a deeper appreciation for the natural world, encourage conservation efforts, and provide meaningful experiences for visitors. By engaging in eco-tourism, travelers can explore pristine ecosystems, participate in educational programs, and support local economies—all while preserving the environment for future generations.

As you embark on your eco-tourism adventure in Sarasota and its surrounding areas, it is essential to remember the principles of responsible travel. By minimizing your environmental impact and promoting sustainable practices, you can ensure that these incredible destinations thrive for future generations. Here are a few tips to keep in mind as you explore the wonders of Sarasota's natural world:

1.   **Leave no trace:** Always carry out any trash you bring and avoid disturbing the natural environment or wildlife. Stick to designated trails and refrain from picking plants or moving rocks.
2.   **Respect local cultures and communities:** Take the time to learn about the history, traditions, and customs of the local communities you visit. Be respectful and considerate of their way of life, and support local businesses whenever possible.
3.   **Conserve water and energy:** Use resources responsibly by conserving water and energy during your stay. Turn off lights, appliances, and faucets when not in use, and consider reusing towels and linens to reduce water waste.
4.   **Choose eco-friendly accommodations and tour operators:** Look for accommodations and tour operators that prioritize sustainable practices and genuinely commit to conservation and community development.
5.   **Spread the word:** Share your eco-tourism experiences with friends, family, and online communities. Raising awareness of these unique destinations and the importance of responsible travel can inspire others to follow in your footsteps and support eco-tourism efforts in Sarasota and beyond.

As you delve into the world of eco-tourism in Sarasota, Florida, you will be amazed by the diverse range of experiences and breathtaking natural beauty that awaits you. From tranquil nature reserves and lush botanical gardens to thrilling outdoor adventures and immersive wildlife encounters, there is something for every eco-conscious traveler to enjoy. By exploring these remarkable destinations, you will create unforgettable memories and contribute to preserving the environment and the well-being of local communities. So, embrace.

the spirit of eco-tourism as you discover the wonders of Sarasota and its surrounding areas.

The Sarasota, Florida, area is a veritable paradise for eco-tourism enthusiasts, offering diverse activities and experiences highlighting the region's unique natural beauty and rich biodiversity. From exploring state parks and protected habitats to learn about marine life conservation, Sarasota provides countless opportunities to immerse yourself in nature while positively impacting the environment.

Myakka River State Park
13208 State Rd 72, Sarasota, FL 34241, USA
Phone:941-361-6511
www.floridastateparks.org/parks-and-trails/myakka-river-state-park

This expansive park covers over 37,000 diverse ecosystems, including wetlands, prairies, and hammocks. Discover its lush scenery by hiking one of the many nature trails, kayaking along the river, or taking a scenic drive. Do not miss the Canopy Walkway for a bird's-eye view of the forest or the Myakka River, home to alligators and various bird species.

Sarasota Bay Estuary Program
111 S Orange Ave Suite 104, Sarasota, FL 34236, USA

the Sarasota Bay, this program offers educational experiences that focus on the region's unique ecosystem. Participate in guided kayak tours and shoreline restoration projects or attend informative workshops to deepen your understanding of the bay's ecology and the importance of conservation.

Marie Selby Botanical Gardens
1534 Mound St, Sarasota, FL 34236, USA
Phone:941-366-5731
www.selby.org/

A stunning 15-acre garden that highlights an impressive collection of rare and exotic plants, including orchids, bromeliads, and other tropical species. Wander through the lush grounds, attend educational programs, or participate in special events while appreciating plant conservation's beauty and importance.

Mote Marine Laboratory & Aquarium
1600 Ken Thompson Pkwy, Sarasota, FL 34236, USA
Phone:941-388-4441
www.mote.org/

This world-renowned research facility and aquarium focus on marine conservation and education. Interact with marine life, attend informative presentations, or participate in eco-friendly programs like beach cleanups and sea turtle nesting patrols to support their conservation efforts.

Oscar Scherer State Park:
1843 S Tamiami Trail, Osprey, FL 34229, USA
Phone:941-483-5956
www.floridastateparks.org/parks-and-trails

Explore this 1,400-acre park's diverse habitats, which include scrubby flatwoods, pine flatwoods, and a rare Florida scrub-jay population. Hike or bike along the park's fifteen miles of trails, paddle along South Creek or participate in ranger-led programs to learn about the area's unique ecosystems.

SARASOTA UNCOVERED

Crowley Museum and Nature Center:
16405 Myakka Rd, Sarasota, FL 34240, USA
Phone:941-322-1000
www.crowleyfl.org/

Located on 190 acres of pristine Florida wilderness, this nature center offers visitors the chance to learn about the region's native flora and fauna through guided tours and interpretive trails. Participate in workshops and special events to deepen your understanding of Florida's natural history and cultural heritage.

Save Our Seabirds:
1708 Ken Thompson Pkwy, Sarasota, FL 34236, USA
Phone:941-388-3010
www.saveourseabirds.org/

A non-profit organization dedicated to rescuing, rehabilitating, and releasing injured birds, Save Our Seabirds offers guided tours of their facilities and educational programs focusing on bird conservation and preserving their habitats.

Historic Spanish Point:
337 N Tamiami Trail, Osprey, FL 34229, USA
Phone:941-966-5214
www.historicspanishpoint.selby.org/

Discover 5,000 years of Florida history at this 30-acre archaeological and environmental museum. Explore preserved shell middens, pioneer homesteads, and stunning gardens while learning about the area's ecological and cultural heritage.

Celery Fields:
6893 Palmer Blvd, Sarasota, FL 34240, USA
Phone:941-861-5000
www.scgov.net/government/parks-recreation-and-natural-resources/find-a-park/celery-fields

Celery Fields, a 360-acre site comprising wetlands, ponds, and marshes, is a haven for birdwatchers and nature enthusiasts. Wander the site's extensive boardwalks and trails to observe various bird species and other wildlife, such as alligators and otters.

Quick Point Nature Reserve
One hundred Gulf of Mexico Dr, Longboat Key, FL 34228, USA
Phone: 941-316-1988
www.longboatkey.org/townhall/departments/parks-recreation

This 34-acre nature reserve on Longboat Key offers a serene escape for visitors exploring the area's diverse coastal habitats. Walk along the winding trails, observe wildlife in their natural surroundings, and learn about preserving these unique ecosystems.

Robinson Preserve
100 Gulf of Mexico Dr, Longboat Key, FL 34228, USA
Phone:941-316-1988
www.longboatkey.org/townhall/departments/parks-recreation

This preserve has 682 acres and features various coastal habitats, including mangroves, salt marshes, and seagrass beds. Explore the area by kayak, hike the trails, or climb the observation tower for stunning views of the surrounding landscape.

SARASOTA UNCOVERED

Rye Preserve:
100 Gulf of Mexico Dr, Longboat Key, FL 34228, USA
Phone:941-316-1988
www.longboatkey.org/townhall/departments/parks-recreation
This 145-acre preserve offers a chance to discover Florida's upland habitats, including pine flatwoods, oak hammocks, and freshwater marshes. Enjoy hiking, picnicking, and wildlife watching, or attend a ranger-led program to learn about the area's ecology.

Lemon Bay Park and Environmental Center
100 Gulf of Mexico Dr, Longboat Key, FL 34228, USA
Phone:941-316-1988
www.longboatkey.org/townhall/departments/parks-recreation
This 210-acre nature park features a mix of mangrove forests, pine flatwoods, and scrub habitats, providing a unique opportunity to learn about Southwest Florida's coastal ecosystems. Enjoy guided nature walks, birdwatching, and educational programs focusing on the area's diverse flora and fauna.

T. Mabry Carlton, Jr. Memorial Reserve
1800 Mabry Carlton Pkwy, Venice, FL 34292, USA
Phone:941-861-5000
www.scgov.net/government/parks-recreation-and-natural-resources/find-a-park/carlton-reserve
Covering over 24,000 acres, this massive reserve offers a chance to explore various habitats, including pine flatwoods, marshes, and hardwood hammocks. Enjoy miles of hiking, biking, and equestrian trails, or participate in guided nature walks and educational programs.

Chapter 6 / Fishing

Fishing is integral to Sarasota's culture, and it is not hard to see why. With its stunning natural beauty, diverse marine life, and accessible fishing spots, Sarasota offers an unparalleled experience for amateur and seasoned anglers. The pristine waters of the Gulf of Mexico, Sarasota Bay, and numerous inland lakes and rivers make it an angler's paradise.

The variety of fishing habitats in the area supports an abundance of fish species, including snook, redfish, tarpon, spotted sea trout, and grouper, among others. Sarasota's warm, subtropical climate makes it an ideal destination for year-round fishing, with each season bringing unique challenges and rewards.

SARASOTA UNCOVERED

One of the reasons people love fishing in Sarasota so much is the variety of fishing experiences available. From offshore fishing in the deep waters of the Gulf of Mexico to inshore fishing in the calm backwaters of Sarasota Bay, there is something for everyone. The area's many piers, jetties, and bridges offer excellent opportunities for land-based fishing, while a plethora of charter services cater to those looking for a guided experience.

Fishing in Sarasota is more than just a sport or a hobby – it is a way of life. The local fishing community is friendly and welcoming, always eager to share their knowledge and passion with visitors. The experience of casting a line in Sarasota's tranquil waters, surrounded by breathtaking scenery and diverse wildlife, is truly unforgettable. It is no wonder that people from all walks of life are drawn to this angling paradise.

Phillippi Estate Park
5500 S Tamiami Trail, Sarasota, FL 34231

This 60-acre oasis along the shores of Phillippi Creek offers a serene setting for fishing enthusiasts to cast their lines and enjoy the great outdoors. The park's scenic waterway is home to various fish species, making it an ideal spot for anglers of all skill levels.

Sarasota Fishing Pier (City Island Park)
1700 Ken Thompson Pkwy, Sarasota, FL 34236

A popular spot for anglers, the Sarasota Fishing Pier offers stunning views of the bay and various fish species. Cast a line and try your luck at catching snook, redfish, and spotted sea trout.

New Pass Fishing Bridge
200 John Ringling Blvd, Sarasota, FL 34236
The New Pass Fishing Bridge is a well-known location for catching snook, redfish, and sheepshead. Enjoy the beautiful surroundings while trying your hand at some fantastic inshore fishing.

South Lido Park
2201 Ben Franklin Dr, Sarasota, FL 34236
South Lido Park features a beautiful beach and a kayak launch, allowing for various fishing experiences. Fish from the shore or venture into the mangrove tunnels for a unique and thrilling adventure.

Blackburn Point Park
421 Blackburn Point Rd, Osprey, FL 34229
Blackburn Point Park offers a serene setting for shoreline fishing, with opportunities to catch redfish, snook, and spotted sea trout. The park also provides a boat ramp for easy access to nearby waters.

Turtle Beach Fishing Pier
8918 Midnight Pass Rd, Sarasota, FL 34242
This quaint fishing pier on Siesta Key offers a peaceful fishing experience with stunning views. Anglers can expect to catch fish, including snapper, sheepshead, and the occasional tarpon.

North Jetty Park
1000 S Casey Key Rd, Nokomis, FL 34275
Located at the Venice Inlet, North Jetty Park is a prime location for fishing enthusiasts. Fish from the rocky jetty or sandy beach, targeting snook, redfish, and other species that frequent the area.

SARASOTA UNCOVERED

Ken Thompson Park
1700 Ken Thompson Pkwy, Sarasota, FL 34236
Description: With its picturesque shoreline and abundant marine life, Ken Thompson Park is a fantastic spot for fishing. Cast your line from the shore or explore the mangroves for a more secluded experience.

Myakka River State Park
13208 State Rd 72, Sarasota, FL 34241
Myakka River State Park offers exceptional freshwater fishing opportunities. Anglers can target largemouth bass, bluegill, and catfish in the park's lakes and the scenic Myakka River.

Oscar Scherer State Park
1843 S Tamiami Trail, Osprey, FL 34229
Oscar Scherer State Park is an angler's paradise home to various freshwater fish species. Cast your line from the park's fishing docks or explore the peaceful waters of South Creek.

Phillippi Estate Park
5500 S Tamiami Trail, Sarasota, FL 34231
Phillippi Estate Park is a serene location for shoreline fishing along the banks of Phillippi Creek. Anglers can enjoy the park's lush surroundings while targeting snook, redfish, and spotted sea trout.

Sarasota Florida Fishing Charters

Sarasota Florida Fishing Charters
2 Marina Plaza, Sarasota, FL 34236
(941) 587-6150   www.sarasota-Florida-fishing-charters.com

Sarasota Florida Fishing Charters provides an exciting and personalized experience for all skill levels by offering inshore, nearshore, and offshore fishing trips targeting various species.

Magic Fishing Adventures
1606 Ken Thompson Pkwy, Sarasota, FL 34236
Phone: (941) 345-7182
www.magicfishingadventures.com

Capt. A USCG licensed and insured captain, Alan Routh offers guided fishing trips aboard his 24-foot Pathfinder. Target species include snook, redfish, tarpon, and more.

Reel Tight Fishing Charters
801 Ken Thompson Pkwy, Sarasota, FL 34236
Phone: (941) 650-7711
www.reeltightfishingcharters.com

Reel Tight Fishing Charters offers inshore and nearshore trips focusing on snook, redfish, tarpon, and more. Capt. Billy Clyde Alstrom is a local expert who can show you the best spots.

Wolfmouth Charters
2 Marina Plaza, Sarasota, FL 34236
(941) 720-4418   www.wolfmouthcharters.com

Specializing in family-friendly fishing experiences, Wolfmouth Charters offers trips targeting various species, including snook, grouper, and kingfish.

SARASOTA UNCOVERED

Chummy Charters
2 Marina Plaza, Sarasota, FL 34236
(941) 812-1598
www.chummycharters.com

Chummy Charters provides a range of fishing experiences, from inshore and backcountry trips to deep-sea adventures targeting grouper, snapper, and amberjack.

Fish-On Charters
190 Taft Dr, Sarasota, FL 34236
(941) 228-3474
www.fishonsarasota.com

Offering inshore, nearshore, and offshore trips, Fish-On Charters targets species such as tarpon, snook, and redfish. Their experienced captain can cater to both beginners and seasoned anglers.

Hooked On Tail Charters
801 Ken Thompson Pkwy, Sarasota, FL 34236
Phone: (941) 587-4906
www.hookedontail.com

Capt. John Tarr offers customized inshore fishing trips, targeting snook, redfish, and trout in Sarasota Bay and surrounding waters. Enjoy a relaxed and friendly atmosphere while fishing.

Rodbender Fishing Charters
801 Ken Thompson Pkwy, Sarasota, FL 34236
Phone: (941) 320-8171   www.rodbender.com

Rodbender Fishing Charters specializes in light tackle and fly fishing, targeting various species in the coastal waters of Sarasota Bay, including snook, redfish, and tarpon.

SiestaKation Charters
2 Marina Plaza, Sarasota, FL 34236
(941) 952-8312   www.siestakationcharters.com

SiestaKation Charters provides inshore and offshore fishing trips and family-friendly eco-tours. Target species include snook, redfish, and grouper.

Reel Addiction Fishing Charters
2 Marina Plaza, Sarasota, FL 34236
Phone: (941) 504-2601
www.reeladdictionfishingcharters.com

Offering inshore and nearshore fishing trips, Reel Addiction Fishing Charters focuses on species such as snook, redfish, and tarpon. They cater to anglers of all experience levels.

SARASOTA UNCOVERED

Chapter 7 / Geocaching

Geocaching is an outdoor recreational activity in which participants use a GPS receiver or mobile device to hide and seek containers, called "geocaches" or "caches," at specific locations marked by coordinates all over the world. It is often described as a game of high-tech hide-and-seek.

A typical geocache is a small, waterproof container containing a logbook where the geocacher can sign their name and date of find. Caches may also have small trinkets or toys, which can be taken or exchanged for something of equal or lesser value. Geocachers are expected to maintain a code of conduct that includes respecting the environment, obeying local laws, and leaving no trace.

To participate in geocaching, one must create an account on a geocaching website, such as Geocaching.com, where geocache locations and information are listed. Participants can search for caches using GPS coordinates, and once they find the cache, they sign the logbook, exchange items if desired, and then log what they find online.

Geocaching has grown in popularity since its inception in 2000, with millions of geocaches hidden worldwide. It is a fun way to explore new locations, enjoy the outdoors, and engage in a global community of enthusiasts.

Geocaching in Sarasota, FL

Geocaching in Sarasota, Florida, offers a unique and exciting way to explore the city's beautiful parks, nature preserves, and hidden gems. With its urban and natural environments, Sarasota provides diverse geocaching experiences for newcomers and seasoned geocachers. The pleasant climate, stunning beaches, and rich cultural heritage make geocaching in Sarasota even more enjoyable.

Popular geocaching spots in Sarasota include nature parks like Myakka River State Park, Oscar Scherer State Park, and the Celery Fields, where you can enjoy scenic trails and diverse wildlife while searching for hidden caches. These parks offer various cache types that require critical thinking skills, from traditional containers to multi-caches and mystery caches.

Urban geocaching in downtown Sarasota allows you to discover historic sites, monuments, and public art installations while searching for cleverly hidden caches. For example, the Marie Selby Botanical Gardens, Bayfront Park, and St. Armands Circle offer a unique blend of nature, culture, and entertainment.

If you are new to geocaching or want to connect with the local geocaching community, consider attending geocaching events in the Sarasota area. These events offer opportunities to gain experience from experienced geocachers, discover new locations, and make new friends who share your passion for this outdoor activity.

SARASOTA UNCOVERED

To start geocaching in Sarasota, create an account on a geocaching website like Geocaching.com, search for caches in the area, and download the coordinates to your GPS device or smartphone app. Remember to follow geocaching etiquette by respecting the environment, obeying local laws, and leaving no trace.

Geocaching in Sarasota, FL, is a fantastic way to experience the city's natural beauty, history, and culture while enjoying a fun and challenging outdoor activity.

Geocaching Community in Sarasota, FL,

Florida Geocaching Association (FGA)
www.floridageocaching.com/
Facebook: www.facebook.com/groups/FloridaGeocachingAssociation/

The Florida Geocaching Association is a statewide organization that connects geocachers in Florida. Their Facebook group is a great place to connect with other geocachers in the Sarasota area.

Southwest Florida Geocachers
www.swflgeocachers.wordpress.com/
Facebook: www.facebook.com/groups/SWFLGeocachers/

The Southwest Florida Geocachers group focuses on geocaching activities in Southwest Florida, including Sarasota and nearby regions. They organize events and share geocaching experiences on their Facebook page.

Tampa Bay Geocaching Store
www.tampabaygeocaching.com/
Phone: (813) 994-2660
Email: support@tampabaygeocaching.com

While not a community per se, the Tampa Bay Geocaching Store is a resource for geocaching enthusiasts in the Tampa Bay area, which is close to Sarasota. They sell geocaching supplies and can be a source of information about geocaching events in the region.

To find geocaching events near Sarasota, visit the Geocaching.com website and follow these steps:

Go to www.geocaching.com/play/search
Click on "Filters" in the top right corner of the map.
In the "Geocache Types" Chapter, select "Event Cache" and deselect other types to display only events.
Enter "Sarasota, FL" in the "Location" field.
Choose a desired search radius (e.g., 10 miles, 20 miles, etc.) in the "Distance" field.
Click "Apply" to display geocaching events within your specified search radius.

Chapter 8 / Golfing

Sarasota, Florida, is truly a golfer's paradise, offering an exceptional array of courses that cater to players of all skill levels. With its pristine white-sand beaches, warm and sunny climate, and lush natural landscapes, this region is a sought-after vacation destination and a haven for golf enthusiasts. The year-round golfing opportunities in Sarasota are unparalleled, as the region's temperate weather allows for enjoyable play no matter the season. Nevertheless, mild winters and sun-soaked summers create the perfect environment for golfers to indulge in their passion at any time of the year.

This vibrant golfing community will offer diverse courses – from prestigious private clubs and gated communities to historic municipal courses and public layouts. Each course offers unique challenges, breathtaking scenery, and top-notch amenities, providing players with an unforgettable golfing experience. In addition, Sarasota's golf courses are meticulously designed and maintained, featuring lush fairways, fast greens, and strategically placed hazards that test your skills and keep you coming back for more.

Golfing in Sarasota immerses you in the area's rich history and culture. Any of the courses have deep historical roots and connections to the legends of the game, such as Bobby Jones and Arnold Palmer, who have graced the fairways and greens of these beautiful layouts. As you tee off in Sarasota, you will follow in the footsteps of golfing greats, adding excitement and prestige to your round.

Sarasota has something for everyone, whether you are a scratch golfer, a casual player, or a beginner looking to learn the game. So, grab your clubs, sunscreen, and shades, and get ready to explore the incredible golfing landscape that awaits you in sunny Sarasota, Florida!

TPC Prestancia ($$$)
4409 Tournament Players Club Dr., Sarasota, FL 34238
(941) 922-2800   www.tpcprestancia.com

This 36-hole facility offers two championship golf courses that Robert von Hagge and Ron Garl designed. In addition, the Stadium Course has hosted several PGA and LPGA tournaments, while the Club Course offers a more forgiving layout for players of all skill levels.

SARASOTA UNCOVERED

The Ritz-Carlton Members Club ($$$$$)
15150 70 Terrace East, Bradenton, FL 34202
(941) 309-2900   www.ritzcarlton.com

Designed by Tom Fazio, this exclusive private club offers an unparalleled golfing experience with pristine course conditions, world-class amenities, and exceptional service. Membership is required for access.

University Park Country Club ($$$)
7671 The Park Blvd., University Park, FL 34201
(941) 359-9999   www.universitypark-fl.com

This 27-hole championship course designed by Ron Garl boasts beautiful, rolling fairways and fast, true greens. The club has received numerous accolades for its superb course conditions and outstanding customer service.

The Concession Golf Club ($$$$)
7700 Lindrick Ln., Bradenton, FL 34202
(941) 322-1922   www.theconcession.com

This Jack Nicklaus and Tony Jacklin-designed course is a true test of skill. With its challenging layout and immaculate greens, The Concession is consistently ranked among the top courses in Florida.

Sara Bay Country Club ($$$)
7011 Willow St., Sarasota, FL 34243
(941) 355-7658   www.sarabaycc.org

Designed by legendary architect Donald Ross, Sara Bay offers a challenging and classic layout with narrow fairways and undulating greens. This private club requires a membership or a member's invitation to play.

Lakewood Ranch Golf and Country Club ($$$)
7650 Legacy Blvd., Lakewood Ranch, FL 34202
(941) 907-4700   www.lakewoodranchgolf.com

Featuring three 18-hole courses designed by Arnold Palmer and Rick Robbins, this country club offers a diverse golfing experience with varying levels of difficulty and unique challenges.

The Meadows Country Club ($$)
3101 Longmeadow, Sarasota, FL 34235
(941) 378-5957   www.meadowscc.org

This club offers three 18-hole courses, each with its distinct character. The Highlands and Meadows courses are more traditional in design, while the Groves is an executive course that offers a faster pace of play.

Laurel Oak Country Club ($$$)
2700 Gary Player Blvd., Sarasota, FL 34240
(941) 378-3608   www.laureloak.com

Home to two 18-hole championship courses designed by Gary Player, this private club offers a challenging and enjoyable golf experience amidst beautiful, natural surroundings.

Bobby Jones Golf Club ($$)
1000 Circus Blvd., Sarasota, FL 34232
(941) 954-4163   www.bobbyjonesgolfclub.com

This historic municipal golf facility offers forty-five holes of golf, including the 18-hole British Course, the 18-hole American Course, and the 9-hole Gillespie Executive Course. The club is named after the legendary golfer Bobby Jones, who played an exhibition match in 1930.

SARASOTA UNCOVERED

Stoneybrook Golf and Country Club ($$$)
8801 Stoneybrook Blvd., Sarasota, FL 34238
(941) 966-2711   www.stoneybrook.net

This Arthur Hills-designed course offers a challenging yet playable layout with beautiful water features and well-placed bunkers. Its impressive amenities include a driving range, practice greens, and a well-stocked pro shop.

Palm Aire Country Club ($$)
5601 Country Club Way, Sarasota, FL 34243
(941) 355-9733   www.palmaire.net

Featuring two 18-hole courses designed by Dick Wilson and Joe Lee, Palm Aire offers various challenges for golfers of all skill levels. For example, the Champion's Course is known for its large, contoured greens, while the Lakes Course boasts stunning water views.

Serenoa Golf Club ($$)
6773 Serenoa Dr., Sarasota, FL 34241
(941) 925-2755   www.serenoagolf.com

Designed by Mark Alden, this 18-hole championship course is known for its well-maintained greens and challenging layout. The course winds through wetlands and natural preserves, providing a serene and picturesque golfing experience.

Bent Tree Country Club ($$)
4700 Bent Tree Blvd., Sarasota, FL 34241
(941) 371-8200   www.benttreecc.net

This semi-private club offers a challenging yet playable course designed by Bill Lewis. With beautiful, tree-lined fairways and well-guarded greens, Bent Tree provides an enjoyable round for golfers of all abilities.

Heritage Oaks Golf and Country Club ($$$)
4800 Chase Oaks Dr., Sarasota, FL 34241
(941) 926-7600   www.heritageoaksgcc.com

This private, gated community features an 18-hole championship golf course designed by Ron Garl. Heritage Oaks offers beautiful fairways, challenging hazards, and well-maintained greens, making it a favorite among local golf enthusiasts.

The Founders Club ($$$$)
3800 Golf Hall Dr., Sarasota, FL 34240
(941) 371-9720   www.thefoundersgolfclub.com

This exclusive, private club boasts a beautiful and challenging 18-hole course designed by Robert Trent Jones Jr. With its limited membership, golfers can enjoy a relaxed and unhurried pace of play on this stunning course.

SARASOTA UNCOVERED

Chapter 9 /.
Hiking Nature Walks

You know, one of the most remarkable ways to experience the natural beauty of Sarasota, Florida, is by taking a hike or going on a nature walk. The area is teeming with lush landscapes, diverse wildlife, and scenic vistas just waiting to be explored. Imagine yourself strolling through a canopy of towering trees, listening to the melodic songs of the birds, and inhaling the fresh, invigorating air. It is like stepping into a vibrant, living postcard!

The best part is that Sarasota offers various hiking and nature walk options, catering to all skill levels and interests. So, Sarasota has you covered whether you are a seasoned hiker looking for a challenging adventure or just someone who wants to enjoy a leisurely walk amid nature's splendor. And nothing beats the feeling of accomplishment and tranquility that comes from spending time outdoors, surrounded by the wonders of nature.

Let me share the top hiking and nature walk venues in the Sarasota area without further ado. Trust me, you will be itching to lace up your boots and hit the trails in no time!

Myakka River State Park ($)
13208 State Road 72, Sarasota, FL 34241
Phone: (941) 361-6511
www.floridastateparks.org/parks-and-trails/myakka-river-state-park

Myakka River State Park is one of Florida's oldest and largest state parks, encompassing over 37,000 acres of diverse ecosystems. The park offers many trails, from easy nature walks to more challenging hikes, ensuring something for everyone.

Oscar Scherer State Park ($)
1843 S Tamiami Trail, Osprey, FL 34229
Phone: (941) 483-5956
www.floridastateparks.org/parks-and-trails/oscar-scherer-state-park

Oscar Scherer State Park is a 1,400-acre park offering various trails, including the popular Lester Finley Barrier-Free Nature Trail, which is wheelchair accessible. The park is also home to the endangered Florida scrub jay.

SARASOTA UNCOVERED

Rothenbach Park (Free)
8650 Bee Ridge Rd, Sarasota, FL 34241
Phone: (941) 861-5000
www.scgov.net/government/parks-recreation-and-natural-resources/find-a-park/rothenbach-park

Rothenbach Park features five miles of paved and unpaved trails winding through diverse habitats. Enjoy a leisurely walk or a more vigorous hike while enjoying the beautiful scenery and wildlife.

Celery Fields (Free)
6893 Palmer Blvd, Sarasota, FL 34240
Phone: (941) 861-5000
www.scgov.net/government/parks-recreation-and-natural-resources/find-a-park/celery-fields

Celery Fields is a 360-acre site that serves as a stormwater collection zone and wildlife habitat. With several miles of trails and boardwalks, it is a fantastic spot for birdwatching and enjoying nature up close.

Red Bug Slough Preserve (Free)
5200 Beneva Rd, Sarasota, FL 34233
Phone: (941) 861-5000
www.scgov.net/government/parks-recreation-and-natural-resources/find-a-park/red-bug-slough-preserve

Red Bug Slough Preserve features seventy-two acres of diverse habitats, including woodlands, wetlands, and a small lake. Several trails, including one that's ADA accessible, meander through the preserve, making it a perfect destination for a peaceful nature walk.

Legacy Trail ($)
Sarasota, FL
Phone: (941) 861-5000
www.scgov.net/government/parks-recreation-and-natural-resources/find-a-park/legacy-trail

Legacy Trail is a 12.5-mile-long paved, multi-use trail from Sarasota to Venice. It is an excellent choice for walking, biking, or jogging while enjoying the picturesque surroundings.

Carlton Reserve (Free)
1800 Mabry Carlton Pkwy, Venice, FL 34292
Phone: (941) 861-5000
www.scgov.net/government/parks-recreation-and-natural-resources/find-a-park/carlton-reserve

Carlton Reserve is a massive 24,565-acre wilderness area with over one hundred miles of trails. The reserve is perfect for hikers seeking a more rugged and remote experience.

Pinecraft Park (Free)
1420 Gilbert Ave, Sarasota, FL 34239
Phone: (941) 861-5000
www.scgov.net/government/parks-recreation-and-natural-resources/find-a-park/pinecraft-park

Pinecraft Park is a small urban oasis with shaded walking paths and a lovely pond. It is a great spot for a tranquil nature walk in the heart of Sarasota.

Heron Creek Forest Preserve (Free)
3400 S Sumter Blvd, North Port, FL 34287
Phone: (941) 861-5000
www.scgov.net/government/parks-recreation-and-natural-resources/find-a-park/heron-creek-forest-preserve

Heron Creek Forest Preserve features 3.5 miles of hiking trails through various habitats, allowing visitors to spot diverse wildlife and experience nature at its finest.

SARASOTA UNCOVERED

Lemon Bay Park and Environmental Center (Free)
570 Bay Park Blvd, Englewood, FL 34223
Phone: (941) 861-5000
www.scgov.net/government/parks-recreation-and-natural-resources/find-a-park/lemon-bay-park-and-environmental-center

Lemon Bay Park offers 210 coastal habitats and a 1.7-mile-long trail system. The park also provides guided nature walks and environmental programs.

Jelks Preserve (Free)
2300 N River Rd, Venice, FL 34292
Phone: (941) 861-5000
www.scgov.net/government/parks-recreation-and-natural-resources/find-a-park/jelks-preserve

Jelks Preserve is a 614-acre haven for wildlife, featuring over eight miles of hiking trails through diverse habitats, including oak hammocks, pine flatwoods, and wetlands.

Sleeping Turtles Preserve North (Free)
3462 Border Rd, Venice, FL 34292
Phone: (941) 861-5000
www.scgov.net/government/parks-recreation-and-natural-resources/find-a-park/sleeping-turtles-preserve-north

Sleeping Turtles Preserve North is a 173-acre property situated along the Myakka River. Its five miles of trails allow visitors to explore various ecosystems and enjoy the riverfront views.

Curry Creek Preserve (Free)
1500 Pinebrook Rd, Venice, FL 34285
Phone: (941) 861-5000
www.scgov.net/government/parks-recreation-and-natural-resources/find-a-park/curry-creek-preserve

Curry Creek Preserve is a 456-acre site with over three miles of trails that take visitors through diverse habitats, such as pine flatwoods, scrubby flatwoods, and mangrove swamps. Keep an eye out for the abundant wildlife that calls the preserve home.

Caspersen Beach Park (Free)
4100 Harbor Dr, Venice, FL 34285
Phone: (941) 861-5000
www.scgov.net/government/parks-recreation-and-natural-resources/find-a-park/caspersen-beach-park

Caspersen Beach Park is known for its pristine shoreline. Still, it also offers a nature trail that winds through coastal habitats, providing a great opportunity to explore the park's unique flora and fauna.

Shamrock Park and Nature Center (Free)
3900 Shamrock Dr, Venice, FL 34293
Phone: (941) 861-5000
www.scgov.net/government/parks-recreation-and-natural-resources/find-a-park/shamrock-park-and-nature-center

Shamrock Park and Nature Center feature eighty acres of diverse habitats, including mangroves, pine flatwoods, and wetlands. The park offers several miles of trails, making it an ideal spot for a leisurely nature walk or a more challenging hike.

SARASOTA UNCOVERED

Chapter 10 /
Horseback Riding

Imagine saddling up on a majestic steed, the warm Florida sun shining as a gentle breeze caressing your face. You are about to journey through Sarasota, Florida's diverse and beautiful landscapes. Horseback riding in this vibrant region offers a unique, exhilarating experience that allows you to connect with nature while exploring the stunning scenery. Whether you are a seasoned equestrian or a beginner just learning the ropes, the thrill of riding through lush forests, sandy beaches, or picturesque trails is an unforgettable adventure that will make your trip to Sarasota truly special.

Sarasota's horseback riding scene has options for riders of all skill levels and interests. From guided trail rides and beachfront gallops to horseback riding lessons and even equestrian therapy programs, there is something for everyone to enjoy. Imagine trotting along the shoreline, the waves lapping at your horse's hooves, or winding your way through a dense forest, the scent of fresh pine filling the air.

The feeling of freedom and connection with your horse and the environment is indescribable, and it is an experience that will undoubtedly make your visit to Sarasota more memorable.

So, if you want to add adventure and excitement to your Sarasota vacation, consider exploring the area on horseback. The region's diverse terrain and abundant riding options make it the perfect destination for equestrians of all ages and skill levels. Just imagine the stories you will be able to share when you return home, regaling friends and family with tales of your thrilling rides through the enchanting landscapes of Sarasota, Florida.

Now, let us dive into the top horseback riding venues in the Sarasota area:

.] Myakka Trail Rides ($$$)
13210 State Rd 72, Sarasota, FL 34241
Phone: (941) 685-8384   www.myakkatrailrides.com

Myakka Trail Rides offers guided horseback trails through the breathtaking Myakka River State Park. Riders of all experience levels can enjoy the park's natural beauty while riding well-trained, gentle horses led by experienced guides.

Deer Prairie Creek Preserve ($$$)
7001 Forbes Trail, Venice, FL 34292
Phone: (941) 485-7011
www.scgov.net/government/parks-recreation-and-natural-resources/find-a-park/deer-prairie-creek-preserve

Deer Prairie Creek Preserve is a 6,400-acre preserve offering horseback riding trails that wind through diverse habitats, including pine flatwoods, oak hammocks, and wetlands. Bring your horse and explore the beautiful trails alone or with friends.

SARASOTA UNCOVERED

Sarasota Polo Club ($$$)
8201 Polo Club Ln, Sarasota, FL 34240
Phone: (941) 907-0000 www.sarasotapolo.com

Sarasota Polo Club offers exciting polo matches during the season and provides riding lessons and clinics for those looking to improve their equestrian skills. Learn from experienced instructors and enjoy the beautiful club grounds.

Hidden Acres Stables ($$)
5700 East Sawgrass Road, Sarasota, FL 34241
Phone: (941) 928-9616 www.hiddenacresstables.com

Hidden Acres Stables offers horseback riding lessons for all ages and abilities, from beginners to advanced riders. With experienced trainers and well-cared-for horses, this family-owned facility provides a welcoming environment for learning and enjoying horseback riding.

Diamond D Ranch ($$$)
12435 Diamond D Ranch Rd, Sarasota, FL 34240
Phone: (941) 371-6791 www.diamonddranch.net

Diamond D Ranch offers various equestrian services, including horse boarding, lessons, and trail rides. With over forty-five acres of lush pastures, riding arenas, and scenic trails, riders can enjoy a serene and picturesque environment for their horseback adventures.

Black Prong Equestrian Village ($$$$)
450 SE County Road 337, Bronson, FL 32621
Phone: (352) 486-1234 www.blackprong.com

Black Prong Equestrian Village is a premier equestrian facility that offers various horse-related activities, including trail rides, riding lessons, and equestrian events. Black Prong is an ideal destination for horse enthusiasts, with over 250 acres of pristine trails and top-notch amenities.

Great World Nature Tours ($$$)
8201 Cooper Creek Blvd, Bradenton, FL 34201
Phone: (941) 720-2916
www.greatworldnaturetours.com

Great World Nature Tours offers guided horseback riding tours for riders of all levels. Explore Florida's natural beauty on well-trained horses, led by knowledgeable and friendly guides who will ensure a safe and enjoyable experience.

Hunsader Farms ($$)
5500 County Rd 675, Bradenton, FL 34211
Phone: (941) 322-2168   www.hunsaderfarms.com

Hunsader Farms is a family-owned farm that offers seasonal horseback riding opportunities during its annual Pumpkin Festival. Enjoy the festive atmosphere and take a leisurely trail ride through the beautiful farm grounds.

Timber Creek Stables ($$$)
5765 Timber Creek Ln, Sarasota, FL 34243
Phone: (941) 359-0399
www.timbercreeksarasota.com

Timber Creek Stables is a full-service equestrian facility that offers horse boarding, riding lessons, and training for riders of all ages and skill levels. With experienced instructors and various well-trained horses, Timber Creek provides a friendly and welcoming environment for equestrian enthusiasts.

Sarasota Riding Academy ($$$)
6201 Rolling Oaks Dr, Sarasota, FL 34240
Phone: (941) 412-9607
www.sarasotaridingacademy.com

Sarasota Riding Academy offers riding lessons for children and adults, focusing on safety, fun, and confidence-building. With experienced trainers and various lesson packages, this academy provides an enjoyable and educational experience for riders of all levels.

SARASOTA UNCOVERED

Myakka River Ranch ($$$)
10460 Saddle Oak Rd, Sarasota, FL 34241
Phone: (941) 312-1123   www.myakkariverranch.com

Myakka River Ranch offers guided horseback trails through the beautiful Myakka River State Park. With experienced guides and gentle horses, riders of all skill levels can enjoy the scenic beauty of the park's diverse ecosystems.

Double R Stables ($$)
2351 Verna Rd, Myakka City, FL 34251
Phone: (941) 322-1501   www.doublerstables.com

Double R Stables is a family-owned and operated facility offering horse boarding, lessons, and trail rides. With a focus on safety and fun, Double R Stables provides a welcoming environment for riders of all ages and skill levels to enjoy horseback riding.

Deer Prairie Creek Preserve ($)
7001 Forbes Trail, Sarasota, FL 34241
Phone: (941) 861-5000   www.scgov.net

Deer Prairie Creek Preserve is a beautiful, natural preserve with over seventy miles of trails perfect for horseback riding. Bring your horse and explore the diverse Florida ecosystems, including pine flatwoods, marshes, and oak hammocks.

Oak Haven Farms ($$$)
13210 State Road 72, Sarasota, FL 34241
Phone: (941) 650-8037   www.oakhavenfarms.net

Oak Haven Farms is a full-service equestrian facility that offers horse boarding, training, and riding lessons. With various well-trained horses and experienced trainers, Oak Haven provides a safe and enjoyable environment for riders of all skill levels.

Chapter 11 /
Kayaking Paddle Board

Imagine gliding through the clear waters of Sarasota, Florida, feeling the sun's warmth on your skin and the gentle breeze on your face. The sound of water splashing against your paddle and seeing wildlife along the shoreline create a symphony of serenity. Whether you are a seasoned paddler or a newcomer to the sport, kayaking, canoeing, and paddleboarding in Sarasota offers a unique perspective on the area's stunning natural beauty.

From the tranquil mangrove tunnels of the Lido Key to the winding waterways of Myakka River State Park, Sarasota boasts an array of paddling experiences that cater to all skill

SARASOTA UNCOVERED

levels and preferences. Drift along serene rivers and estuaries, or challenge yourself with a coastal paddle along the Gulf of Mexico. As you explore these beautiful waterways, you may encounter dolphins, manatees, and

various bird species. Let the beauty of nature envelop you as you embark on an unforgettable aquatic adventure.

Remember, before you embark on your aquatic adventure, it is crucial to prioritize safety. Always practice safe water sports by wearing a flotation device and ensuring everyone participating in the activity has one. Remember, safety comes first! By taking these precautions, you can enjoy a memorable and worry-free journey through the sparkling waters of Sarasota, Florida, and experience the magic of its aquatic wonderland firsthand.

Economy Tackle/Dolphin Paddle Sports ($$)
6018 S Tamiami Trail, Sarasota, FL 34231
Phone: (941) 922-9671   www.floridakayak.com/

Economy Tackle/Dolphin Paddle Sports offers kayak, canoe, paddleboard rentals, sales, and guided tours. Explore Sarasota's waterways at your own pace or join a guided tour to discover the area's hidden gems with the help of experienced guides.

Lido Key Mangrove Tunnels ($$)
190 Taft Dr, Sarasota, FL 34236
Phone: (941) 346-0891   www.kayakfl.com/

Lido Key Mangrove Tunnels provides guided kayak tours through the breathtaking mangrove tunnels of Lido Key. Navigate through a labyrinth of lush, green tunnels teeming with wildlife, including birds, fish, and manatees.

Myakka River State Park ($)
13208 State Rd 72, Sarasota, FL 34241
Phone: (941) 361-6511   www.floridastateparks.org

Myakka River State Park offers canoe, kayak, and paddleboard rentals for paddlers exploring the park's fifty-eight square miles of wetlands, hammocks, and prairies. Paddle along the picturesque Myakka River or navigate the park's diverse ecosystems.

Sarasota Paddleboard Company ($$$)
1051 Longboat Club Rd, Longboat Key, FL 34228
Phone: (941) 301-8776
www.sarasotapaddleboardcompany.com/

Sarasota Paddleboard Company specializes in paddleboard rentals, lessons, and guided tours. With a focus on safety and fun, they provide paddlers with top-quality equipment and knowledgeable guides to ensure an enjoyable experience on the water.

Ted Sperling Park at South Lido Beach ($)
2201 Benjamin Franklin Dr, Sarasota, FL 34236
Phone: (941) 861-5000   www.scgov.net/

Ted Sperling Park at South Lido Beach is a popular kayaking, canoeing, and paddleboarding launch site. Paddle through mangrove tunnels or along the park's shoreline, where you may spot Dolphins, manatees, and various bird species.

Siesta Key Paddleboards ($$$)
Siesta Key, FL
Phone: (941) 301-8776
www.siestakeypaddleboards.com/

Siesta Key Paddleboards offers paddleboard rentals, guided tours, and lessons for visitors of all skill levels. Explore the beautiful waters around Siesta Key and discover the area's diverse marine life and picturesque scenery.

SARASOTA UNCOVERED

Kayaking SRQ Tours & Rentals ($$$)
Ted Sperling Park, 190 Taft Dr, Sarasota, FL 34236
Phone: (941) 799-1863   www.kayakingsrq.com/

Kayaking SRQ Tours & Rentals specializes in guided eco-tours and kayak rentals, providing fun, educational, and memorable experiences. Discover Sarasota's waterways and wildlife as you paddle through mangrove tunnels and estuaries.

Liquid Blue Outfitters ($$$)
1605 Ken Thompson Pkwy, Sarasota, FL 34236
Phone: (941) 896-7884   www.liquid-blue-outfitters.com/

Liquid Blue Outfitters offers kayak and paddleboard rentals, guided tours, and lessons in Sarasota's beautiful waters. Their experienced guides will help you navigate the area's waterways and share their knowledge about the local ecosystem.

Almost Heaven Kayak Adventures ($$$)
190 Taft Dr, Sarasota, FL 34236
Phone: (941) 504-6296   www.kayakfl.com/

Almost Heaven Kayak Adventures offers guided kayak tours that explore the beauty and serenity of Sarasota's waterways. Paddle through mangrove tunnels, estuaries, and coastal waters while encountering various wildlife.

Island Jet Ski Tours & Rentals ($$$)
200 Bridge St, Bradenton Beach, FL 34217
Phone: (941) 254-2311   www.islandjetski.com/

Island Jet Ski Tours & Rentals provides kayak, paddleboard, jet ski rentals, and guided tours. Explore the waters of Sarasota and the surrounding barrier islands with the help of their knowledgeable guides.

Happy Paddler Kayak Tours & EcoVentures ($$$)
Sarasota, FL
Phone: (941) 773-1920   www.happypaddler.com/

Happy Paddler Kayak Tours & EcoVentures offers guided kayak tours in Sarasota, focused on providing eco-friendly and educational experiences. Paddle through mangroves, estuaries, and coastal waters while learning about the local ecosystem.

Paradise Adventures ($$$)
Sarasota, FL
Phone: (941) 275-2971
www.paradiseadventuresfl.com/

Paradise Adventures offers guided kayak and paddleboard tours in the Sarasota area. Discover the beauty of Sarasota's waterways as you paddle through mangroves, estuaries, and along the coastline with the help of experienced guides.

Silent Sports Outfitters ($$$)
2301 N Tamiami Trail, Nokomis, FL 34275
Phone: (941) 966-5477
www.silentsportsoutfitters.com/

Silent Sports Outfitters offers kayak, canoe, paddleboard rentals, sales, and guided tours in the Sarasota area. Explore the region's waterways and natural beauty with top-quality equipment and experienced guides.

SUP Sarasota ($$$)
Sarasota, FL
Phone: (941) 504-1699   www.supsarasota.com/

SUP Sarasota specializes in stand-up paddleboard rentals, lessons, and guided tours. Focusing on safety, fun, and adventure, they provide paddlers with top-quality equipment and experienced guides to ensure an unforgettable experience on the water.

SARASOTA UNCOVERED

Chapter 12 /
Family Fun With Kids

I can tell you are on the hunt for the ultimate family vacation, a place that offers exciting and memorable experiences for everyone, especially the little ones. Well, search no more because I've your dream destination. Just picture this: soft, powdery white-sand beaches perfect for sandcastle-building; fascinating museums that will ignite your kids' curiosity and imagination; and lush botanical gardens where families can explore and learn together, eagerly awaiting your arrival.

You guessed it; we are talking about Sarasota, Florida, an absolute gem on the Gulf Coast that offers the perfect fusion of relaxation, adventure, and family fun. Envision Sarasota as a treasure chest overflowing with delightful experiences designed to delight kids and grown-ups alike. Each activity is a sparkling jewel just waiting to be discovered, and the memories you make will be priceless keepsakes you will cherish for years to come.

So, let us dive into the enchanting world of Sarasota and uncover the best family-friendly venues where adventure, learning, and laughter come together to create the perfect family vacation. As we explore these fantastic spots, you will see how much this coastal paradise has in store for families. From interactive exhibits that spark young minds to thrilling outdoor adventures that encourage teamwork and bonding, Sarasota offers an unforgettable journey for kids and grown-ups alike.

Prepare to embark on a voyage of discovery, where your family's shared experiences will become the cherished gems in your treasure chest of memories. It is time to uncover Sarasota's magic and see why this vibrant and welcoming city is truly the ultimate family vacation destination.

Mote Marine Laboratory & Aquarium - $$
1600 Ken Thompson Pkwy, Sarasota, FL 34236
Phone: (941) 388-4441   www.mote.org/

Dive into the fascinating world of marine life at this renowned research institution and aquarium. Get up close and personal with sharks, sea turtles, and more while fostering a love for ocean conservation in your little ones.

SARASOTA UNCOVERED

Marie Selby Botanical Gardens - $$$
900 S Palm Ave, Sarasota, FL 34236
Phone: (941) 366-5731 www.selby.org/

Stroll through the enchanting gardens that feel like a tropical paradise, where rare orchids and lush foliage create a serene oasis for families to explore and appreciate nature's beauty.

The Ringling - $$$
5401 Bay Shore Rd, Sarasota, FL 34243
Phone: (941) 359-5700 www.ringling.org/

Step into a world of art, history, and circus magic at the former home of John and Mable Ringling. From the majestic Ca' d'Zan mansion to the Circus Museum, something here captivates everyone's imagination.

Sarasota Jungle Gardens - $$
3701 Bay Shore Rd, Sarasota, FL 34234
Phone: (941) 355-5305
www.sarasotajunglegardens.com/

Get up close and personal with Florida's native wildlife at this family-friendly attraction. Feed flamingos, watch interactive animal shows, and wander the lush gardens for an unforgettable experience.

Siesta Key Beach - Free
Siesta Beach, 948 Beach Rd, Sarasota, FL 34242
www.scgov.net/beaches

Sink your toes into the powdery white sands of Siesta Key Beach, rated one of the best beaches in the United States. Perfect for a relaxing day of sun, sand, and surf with the whole family.

Big Cat Habitat and Gulf Coast Sanctuary - $$
7101 Palmer Blvd, Sarasota, FL 34240
Phone: (941) 371-6377   www.bigcathabitat.org/

Witness majestic lions, tigers, and other big cats up close at this sanctuary dedicated to rescuing and providing a forever home to these incredible animals. Interactive shows and animal encounters make this a must-visit.

Myakka River State Park - $
13208 State Rd 72, Sarasota, FL 34241
Phone: (941) 361-6511   www.floridastateparks.org

Escape to the wild side of Florida and explore the diverse ecosystems of Myakka River State Park. Hike, bike, or kayak through the park, and watch for alligators, birds, and other native wildlife.

Children's Garden & Art Center - $$
1670 10th Way, Sarasota, FL 34236
Phone: (941) 330-1711
www.sarasotasucculentcircle.com/

Let your kids' imaginations run wild in this whimsical garden filled with interactive play areas, creative sculptures, and delightful art installations designed to inspire a love of nature and art.

Sarasota Classic Car Museum - $$
5500 N Tamiami Trl, Sarasota, FL 34243
Phone: (941) 355-6228
www.sarasotacarmuseum.org/

Travel back in time as you explore an impressive collection of vintage automobiles and memorabilia. This museum is perfect for car enthusiasts and history buffs alike.

SARASOTA UNCOVERED

The Bishop Museum of Science and Nature - $$
201 10th St W, Bradenton, FL 34205
Phone: (941) 746-4131   www.bishopscience.org/

Uncover the wonders of science, history, and the cosmos at this interactive museum. From a state-of-the-art planetarium to engaging exhibits, there is something for every curious mind.

Urban Air Trampoline and Adventure Park - $$$
6180 Edgelake Dr, Sarasota, FL 34240
Phone: (941) 413-5127
www.urbanairtrampolinepark.com

Jump into a world of fun at this indoor adventure park featuring trampolines, obstacle courses, and more, providing endless excitement for the whole family.

TreeUmph! Adventure Course - $$$
21805 E State Rd 70, Bradenton, FL 34202
Phone: (941) 322-2130   www.treeumph.com/

Reach new heights as you navigate treetop obstacle courses, zip lines, and swinging bridges. This exhilarating adventure is perfect for families with a taste for excitement.

Florida Maritime Museum - Free
4415 119th St W, Cortez, FL 34215
Phone: (941) 708-6120
www.floridamaritimemuseum.org/

Discover Florida's rich maritime history at this captivating museum, where exhibits on boatbuilding, fishing, and more bring the state's nautical heritage to life.

Payne Park Skate Park - $
2050 Adams Ln, Sarasota, FL 34237
Phone: (941) 263-8383   www.letsplaysarasota.com

Unleash your inner skater at this top-notch skate park, offering ramps, bowls, and rails suitable for all skill levels.

Smugglers Cove Adventure Golf - $$
3815 N Tamiami Trl, Sarasota, FL 34234
Phone: (941) 351-6620   www.smugglersgolf.com/

Put your way through a pirate-themed mini-golf course with waterfalls, caves, and live alligators. A fun-filled activity that the entire family will treasure.

In Conclusion

So, there you have it, my friend! Sarasota, Florida, is a treasure trove of family fun waiting to be discovered. From the sun-kissed shores of Siesta Key Beach to the enchanting world of The Ringling, there is something to delight every family member. Sarasota has it all, whether you are seeking thrilling adventure, engaging education, or a peaceful retreat into nature. Just imagine the memories you will create as you explore the wonders of the marine world, conquer treetop obstacle courses, or uncover the state's rich history. The possibilities are as vast as the sands on the beach, so why wait? Start planning your family's unforgettable Sarasota vacation today and let the treasure hunt for lifelong memories begin.!

Chapter 13 / Wildlife and Bird Watching

So, you are looking for a getaway to immerse yourself in nature, lose yourself in the symphony of birdsong, and witness the wonders of wildlife up close. Well, let me tell you about a little slice of paradise that will satisfy your cravings for adventure and tranquility. Imagine a place where azure waters meet emerald landscapes, myriad bird species dance across the sky, and wildlife roams free, just waiting for you to discover their secrets. This magical haven in Sarasota, Florida, is a true gem on the Gulf Coast, offering abundant opportunities for wildlife viewing and birdwatching enthusiasts.

Picture Sarasota as a living, breathing canvas painted with the vibrant colors of flora and fauna, where each brushstroke reveals a new and fascinating creature. Like a treasure map, the city and its surrounding areas are dotted with hidden gems. You can embark on a journey of discovery to witness the incredible diversity of life that calls this region home. From the playful antics of manatees and dolphins to the serene beauty of migratory birds, Sarasota's natural wonders promise to leave you awestruck and yearning for more.

As we embark on this adventure, let me guide you to the fifteen best wildlife viewing and birdwatching venues in the Sarasota area. I will lead you through pristine nature reserves, lush wetlands, and enchanting parks, each offering unique opportunities to observe and appreciate the captivating world of wildlife. Along the way, you will deepen your connection with nature and create unforgettable memories you will cherish forever.

So, grab your binoculars, lace up your hiking boots, and get ready to embark on a thrilling journey into the heart of Sarasota's natural wonders. As we explore these remarkable venues, you will discover that the city's treasures extend far beyond its sparkling beaches and vibrant arts scene, inviting you to experience the wild side of Florida like never before.

Myakka River State Park - $$
13208 State Road 72, Sarasota, FL 34241
Phone: (941) 361-6511   www.floridastateparks.org

A vast, pristine wilderness with diverse ecosystems, Myakka River State Park offers a true immersion into Florida's natural beauty. The park's extensive trail system and birding boardwalks provide many opportunities to spot native birds and wildlife, including alligators, deer, and countless bird species.

SARASOTA UNCOVERED

Celery Fields: Price Free
6893 Palmer Blvd, Sarasota, FL 34240
Phone: (941) 861-5000   www.scgov.net

A haven for birdwatchers, Celery Fields features restored wetlands that attract over two hundred bird species. Wander the trails, climb the observation mound, and visit the Audubon Nature Center to learn more about the area's avian residents, including the elusive purple gallinule and roseate spoonbill.

Mote Marine Laboratory & Aquarium - Price: $$$$
1600 Ken Thompson Pkwy, Sarasota, FL 34236
Phone: (941) 388-4441   www.mote.org/

Discover the wonders of marine life at Mote Marine Laboratory & Aquarium. Get up close with manatees, sea turtles, and sharks, and explore the outdoor habitats of various coastal birds. With a focus on research and conservation, Mote offers an educational and engaging experience for wildlife enthusiasts of all ages.

Oscar Scherer State Park - $
1843 S Tamiami Trail, Osprey, FL 34229
Phone: (941) 483-5956   www.floridastateparks.org

Nestled within a rare scrubby flatwood ecosystem, Oscar Scherer State Park is a birdwatcher's paradise. The park provides critical habitat for the threatened Florida scrub-jay and offers miles of hiking trails where you may also spot bald eagles, ospreys, and an array of other native birds.

Sarasota Jungle Gardens - $$$
3701 Bay Shore Rd, Sarasota, FL 34234
Phone: (941) 355-5305
www.sarasotajunglegardens.com/

A family favorite, Sarasota Jungle Gardens offers an intimate wildlife experience. Stroll through lush tropical landscapes while observing free-roaming flamingos, parrots, and other exotic birds. Do not miss the interactive animal shows, where you can learn about fascinating creatures worldwide.

Marie Selby Botanical Gardens: Price $$$$
1534 Mound St, Sarasota, FL 34236
Phone: (941) 366-5731   www.selby.org/

Marie Selby Botanical Gardens boasts a stunning collection of plants and various bird species attracted to the lush vegetation. Wander through the gardens, watching for the numerous birds that make their home here, including herons, egrets, and vibrant songbirds.

Lemon Bay Park and Environmental Center: Price: Free
570 Bay Park Blvd, Englewood, FL 34223
Phone: (941) 861-5000   www.scgov.net

Lemon Bay Park and Environmental Center offer a peaceful birdwatching and wildlife-viewing retreat. The park features a mix of habitats, including mangroves and scrubs, providing a home for numerous bird species, gopher tortoises, and even the occasional bobcat. Explore the park's scenic trails and take in the beauty of nature.

Robinson Preserve: Price: Free
1704 99th St NW, Bradenton, FL 34209
Phone: (941) 742-5923   www.mymanatee.org

Robinson Preserve is a sprawling natural area teeming with wildlife, including many birds, such as roseate spoonbills and white pelicans. Traverse the preserve's extensive trail network, kayak through the mangroves, or climb the observation tower for panoramic views and excellent birdwatching opportunities.

SARASOTA UNCOVERED

Quick Point Nature Reserve: Price: Free
One hundred Gulf of Mexico Dr, Longboat Key, FL 34228
Phone: (941) 316-1988   www.longboatkey.org

Nestled on Longboat Key, Quick Point Nature Reserve offers a serene setting for wildlife enthusiasts. Wander the winding trails through diverse habitats, where you may spot wading birds, shorebirds, and even the occasional manatee. The park's boardwalks and observation areas provide excellent vantage points for birdwatching and photography.

Jiggs Landing PreservePrice: - $
6106 63rd St E, Bradenton, FL 34203
Phone: (941) 748-4501   www.mymanatee.org

Jiggs Landing Preserve on the Braden River is ideal for birdwatching and wildlife viewing. Rent a kayak or canoe and explore the river, watching for wading birds, ospreys, and even playful otters. The preserve's peaceful setting makes it a perfect destination for a day spent connecting with nature.

Carlton Reserve: Price: Free
1800 Mabry Carlton Pkwy, Venice, FL 34292
Phone: (941) 861-5000   www.scgov.net/

Carlton Reserve is a massive wilderness area offering various habitats for wildlife and birdwatching enthusiasts. Explore the park's numerous trails, where you may encounter wild turkeys, wading birds, and even the occasional Florida panther. The reserve's diverse ecosystems make it a favorite among nature lovers and birdwatchers.

Heron Creek Forest Price: Free
5201 Heron Creek Blvd, North Port, FL 34287
Phone: (941) 861-5000   www.scgov.net

Heron Creek Forest is a hidden gem offering exceptional birdwatching and wildlife viewing opportunities. The park's thick vegetation and wetland areas provide a refuge for various bird species, including wading birds and songbirds. Hike the trails, and you may even spot deer or other elusive wildlife.

Potter Park: -. $
8587 Potter Park Dr, Sarasota, FL 34238
Phone: (941) 861-5000   www.scgov.net/gov

Potter Park is a peaceful oasis with natural habitats and recreational amenities. The park's pond and wetland areas attract various bird species, making it a great spot for birdwatching. Families can also enjoy the park's playground, picnic areas, and sports facilities, making it a perfect destination for a day outdoors.

Pinecraft Park Price: Price Free
1420 Gilbert Ave, Sarasota, FL 34239
Phone: (941) 861-5000   www.scgov.net

Pinecraft Park is a small urban park with a serene setting that attracts various bird species. Stroll the park's walking paths, relax under the shade of mature trees, and watch for the many birds that make their home here. Pinecraft Park offers a quiet retreat for birdwatching and relaxation within the city.

Red Bug Slough Reserve Price: Free
5200 Beneva Rd, Sarasota, FL 34233
Phone: (941) 861-5000   www.scgov.net

Red Bug Slough Reserve is a 72-acre preserve that provides a habitat for various bird species and other wildlife. The reserve features hiking trails, a butterfly garden, and a picturesque slough. Visitors can enjoy birdwatching, photography, and this natural oasis's peaceful surroundings in Sarasota's heart.

SARASOTA UNCOVERED

Chapter 14 / Casino Gambling

Roll the Dice: A Guide to Casino Gambling in Sarasota, Florida

Imagine yourself in the heart of Sarasota, Florida, with the sun setting over the horizon as you prepare for an exciting night out. The anticipation builds as you step into a world of glitz and glamour, where luck and skill intertwine, and fortunes are won and lost with the roll of a dice or the spin of a wheel. Welcome to the thrilling world of casino gambling in Sarasota, where you can test your luck, indulge in fine dining, and enjoy live entertainment all under one roof.

Sarasota's casinos offer various gaming options to suit your tastes, whether you are a high roller, a casual gambler, or simply seeking a night of fun and excitement. From the classic charm of the roulette wheel to the fast-paced action of the craps table, the allure of blackjack, and the bright lights and sounds of slot machines, there is something for everyone. As you immerse yourself in this exciting world, you will also discover a wide variety of dining options, ranging from elegant gourmet restaurants to casual buffets, as well as live shows and performances catering to various interests.

As you embark on your casino adventure in Sarasota, remember that responsible gambling is critical to ensuring an enjoyable experience. Set limits on your spending and remember that the primary goal is to have fun. With a touch of Lady Luck on your side and a spirit of excitement, you are sure to create unforgettable memories as you explore the vibrant casino scene in Sarasota, Florida.

One-Eyed Jacks Poker Room ($$)
5400 Bradenton Rd, Sarasota, FL 34234
Phone: (941) 355-7744   www.skcpoker.com/

One-Eyed Jacks Poker Room offers various poker games, including Texas Hold'em, Omaha, and Seven Card Stud. The venue is renowned for its friendly atmosphere and professional staff, making it an ideal choice for novice and experienced poker players.

Sarasota Kennel Club ($$)
5400 Bradenton Rd, Sarasota, FL 34234
Phone: (941) 355-7744   www.sarasotakennelclub.com

Sarasota Kennel Club is a historic racing and gaming facility that offers live greyhound racing, simulcast wagering, and a poker room. Enjoy the thrill of live racing, place your bets, or try poker in the club's lively atmosphere.

Tropical Breeze Casino ($$$)
7917 Bayshore Dr, Port Richey, FL 34668
Phone: (844) 386-2789   www.portricheycasino.com/

Tropical Breeze Casino is a casino cruise ship that offers various table games, including blackjack, roulette, and craps, as well as over one hundred slot machines. Enjoy the excitement of casino gaming while taking in stunning views of the Gulf of Mexico.

SARASOTA UNCOVERED

The Casino Beach Bar ($$)
25000 Tamiami Trail E, Naples, FL 34114
Phone: (239) 394-2511   www.casinobeachbar.com/

The Casino Beach Bar is a laid-back beachside venue that offers slot machines, video poker, and electronic blackjack. Sip on a tropical cocktail

Victory Casino Cruises ($$$)
180 Christopher Columbus Dr, Cape Canaveral, FL 32920
Phone: (855) 468-4286   www.victorycasinocruises.com

Victory Casino Cruises offers a Vegas-style casino experience on the water. You will be spoilt for choice with over six hundred slot machines, blackjack, craps, roulette, poker, and more. Enjoy live entertainment, fine dining, and breathtaking ocean views as you sail on this exhilarating casino cruise.

In Conclusion

As the sun sets on your Sarasota adventure, reflect on the excitement, glamour, and thrill of the casino gambling scene you have explored. From the intensity of a high-stakes poker game to the anticipation of the roulette wheel, the dazzling lights and sounds of slot machines, to the live shows and performances, Sarasota's casinos offer a unique and unforgettable experience. As you reflect on your time in this vibrant city, you will have memories to cherish and stories to share with friends and family while eagerly anticipating your next visit to the casino wonderland of Sarasota, Florida.

Remember, whether you are a seasoned gambler or new to the scene, responsible gambling is essential for an enjoyable experience. Set limits, have fun, and embrace the spirit of excitement that permeates the air in Sarasota's casinos. With luck and a sense of adventure, you will be drawn into the captivating casino gambling world, creating memories that will last a lifetime.

Chapter 15 / City tours

Picture yourself strolling through the charming streets of Sarasota, Florida, as the sun casts a warm glow on the historic buildings and lush greenery. The city's rich cultural heritage, vibrant arts scene, and stunning natural beauty create a tapestry of unforgettable experiences. To truly immerse yourself in the wonders of this enchanting city, embark on a guided city tour that will not only reveal its hidden gems but also allow you to see Sarasota through the eyes of a local. From fascinating historical landmarks to breathtaking gardens and parks, each tour offers a unique perspective on the essence of Sarasota.

Whether you are an art lover, a history buff, or an outdoor enthusiast, Sarasota's diverse city tours cater to a wide range of interests and passions. With expert guides eager to share their knowledge and stories, you will better appreciate the

SARASOTA UNCOVERED

city's vibrant past and present and future aspirations. So, grab your walking shoes, hop on a trolley, or set sail on a scenic cruise and let the adventure unfold before you. As you explore the city's many facets, you will create memories that will last a lifetime and even uncover your connection to Sarasota, Florida.

Discover Sarasota Tours ($$)
1826 4th St, Sarasota, FL 34236
Phone: (941) 260-9818
www.discoversarasotatours.com/

Discover Sarasota Tours offers various guided trolley and walking tours that explore the city's history, culture, and natural beauty. From historic neighborhoods to haunted sites, public art to circus history, there is a tour for every interest and taste.

Sarasota Suncoast Tours ($$$)
Sarasota, FL
Phone: (941) 363-9556
www.sarasotasuncoasttours.com/

Sarasota Suncoast Tours specializes in private and customizable tours, providing visitors with an intimate and personalized experience. Explore the city's best attractions, hidden gems, and local favorites with knowledgeable guides catering to your interests.

LeBarge Tropical Cruises ($$$)
2 Marina Plaza, Sarasota, FL 34236
Phone: (941) 366-6116
www.lebargetropicalcruises.com/

LeBarge Tropical Cruises offers a unique perspective in Sarasota with its floating island cruise. Enjoy a narrated sightseeing tour of Sarasota Bay, the beautiful waterfront homes, and marine wildlife while relaxing in a tropical paradise on the water.

Around the Bend Nature Tours ($$)
P.O. Box 14355, Bradenton, FL 34280
Phone: (941) 794-8773
www.aroundbend.com/

Around the Bend Nature Tours combines adventure with education, offering guided eco-tours that delve into Sarasota's diverse ecosystems, wildlife, and history. Explore parks, preserves, and archaeological sites with experienced naturalists who share their passion for the region.

Sarasota Opera House Tours ($)
61 N Pineapple Ave, Sarasota, FL 34236
Phone: (941) 328-1300
www.sarasotaopera.org/opera-house-tours

Sarasota Opera House Tours provide a behind-the-scenes look at the iconic venue, highlighting its stunning architecture, history, and artistic heritage. Learn about the fascinating stories and legends that have graced its stage and the ongoing efforts to preserve and enhance this cultural treasure.

In Conclusion

As you wrap up your tour of Sarasota, you will leave with a newfound appreciation for the city's vibrant history, breathtaking landscapes, and enduring spirit. Each of the tours listed above offers a unique window into the heart and soul of Sarasota, revealing its many layers, secrets, and treasures. From the historic neighborhoods to the azure waters of Sarasota Bay, the city's captivating charm is bound to leave a lasting impression.

Whether you choose to dive deep into Sarasota's rich cultural heritage or explore its lush natural surroundings, you will be swept away by the beauty and warmth of this enchanting Florida gem. So, take the time

SARASOTA UNCOVERED

to truly experience Sarasota—venture off the beaten path, engage with the locals, and savor every moment. In doing so, you will not only create unforgettable memories but also forge a deep and lasting connection with the city that will beckon you back time and time again.

As you plan your journey through Sarasota, remember that each tour is a doorway to discovery, an invitation to step into the city's fascinating past, present, and future. Embrace the adventure and let the spirit of Sarasota guide you on a captivating and unforgettable journey that will linger long after you have returned home.

Chapter 16 / Historical Sites

Sarasota, Florida, renowned for its stunning beaches, vibrant arts scene, and lush natural beauty, is also steeped in history. As you explore its streets, parks, and shores, you will discover a treasure trove of stories waiting to be told. From ancient Native American settlements to the pioneers of the late 19th century and the visionaries of the 20th century, Sarasota's history is a fascinating tapestry that weaves together diverse threads of culture, architecture, and human ingenuity. Whether you are a history buff or a casual traveler seeking a deeper understanding of the region, Sarasota's historical sites offer a window into the city's rich and varied past.

As you journey through the annals of Sarasota's history, you will encounter intriguing characters, including intrepid

SARASOTA UNCOVERED

settlers, artists, and entrepreneurs, who have shaped the city's identity and left an

indelible mark on its landscape. From beautifully preserved homes and buildings to archaeological sites and museums, Sarasota's historical landmarks offer a captivating glimpse into the lives of those who came before us, inviting you to connect with the city more intimately.

To help you embark on your historical journey through Sarasota, we have compiled a list of the top historical sites in the area. These destinations will provide enlightenment, enjoyment, and a deeper appreciation of the city's remarkable heritage.

Historic Spanish Point ($$)
337 N. Tamiami Trail, Osprey, FL 34229
Phone: (941) 966-5214
www.historicspanishpoint.org/

Historic Spanish Point is a 30-acre archaeological, historical, and environmental museum. The site features prehistoric shell middens, a pioneer homestead, and beautifully maintained gardens.

Cà d'Zan Mansion at The Ringling ($$)
5401 Bay Shore Rd, Sarasota, FL 34243
Phone: (941) 359-5700
www.ringling.org/ca-dzan

Cà d'Zan Mansion is the opulent former home of circus magnate John Ringling and his wife, Mable. This Venetian Gothic-style mansion offers guided tours and stunning views of Sarasota Bay.

Sarasota County History Center ($)
701 N. Tamiami Trail, Sarasota, FL 34236
Phone: (941) 361-2453
www.sarasotahistoryalive.com/

The Sarasota County History Center offers a wealth of information on local history through exhibits, archives, and interactive displays, providing an in-depth look at the region's past.

Mote Marine Laboratory & Aquarium ($$)
1600 Ken Thompson Pkwy, Sarasota, FL 34236
Phone: (941) 388-4441   www.mote.org/

Mote Marine Laboratory & Aquarium's origins date back to 1955. It exhibits the region's marine life and history, a working research lab, and a 135,000-gallon shark habitat.

Whitaker Gateway Park ($)
1455 N. Tamiami Trail, Sarasota, FL 34236
Phone: (941) 263-6386
www.letsplaysarasota.com

Whitaker Gateway Park is home to the historic Whitaker Family Cemetery, dating back to the 1800s. The park also features walking trails, picnic areas, and a playground, making it a perfect spot to explore Sarasota's history and enjoy the outdoors.

Historic Asolo Theater
5401 Bay Shore Rd, Sarasota, FL 34243
Phone: (941) 359-5700   www.ringling.org

Description: The Historic Asolo Theater, located within the John and Mable Ringling Museum of Art, is a beautifully restored 18th-century Italian theater. Its ornate design and intimate setting make it a unique venue for live performances and a must-see attraction for history and art enthusiasts.

SARASOTA UNCOVERED

Marietta Museum of Art & Whimsy
2121 N Tamiami Trail, Sarasota, FL 34234
Phone: (941) 364-3399
www.whimsymuseum.org

Description: This quirky museum houses a fascinating collection of art, whimsical sculptures, and artifacts highlighting the region's creative spirit. The eclectic mix of works in a lush garden setting offers a lighthearted glimpse into the area's artistic history.

The Powel Crosley Estate
8374 N Tamiami Trail, Sarasota, FL 34243
Phone: (941) 722-3244
www.powelcrosleyestate.com

Description: Built-in 1929, the Powel Crosley Estate is a stunning example of Mediterranean Revival architecture. Once the winter home of Powel Crosley Jr., an inventor, and entrepreneur, this meticulously restored mansion is now a popular venue for events and weddings and offers guided tours.

Sarasota Classic Car Museum
5500 N Tamiami Trail, Sarasota, FL 34243
Phone: (941) 355-6228
www.sarasotacarmuseum.org

Description: The Sarasota Classic Car Museum is a must-visit for automobile enthusiasts. It features over one hundred vintage cars, from sleek sports cars to elegant luxury vehicles, providing a fascinating look into the history of the automobile industry.

Newtown Alive Sarasota, FL 34234
(Tours begin at Dr. Martin Luther King Jr. Park)
Phone: (941) 260-9193
www.newtownalive.org

Description: Newtown Alive is an initiative dedicated to preserving and sharing the history of Sarasota's African American community. It offers guided walking tours through the Newtown neighborhood, highlighting its rich cultural heritage and historical landmarks.

Chapter 17 / Movie Theater

Movie theaters have a certain charm and allure that is hard to resist. From the hushed anticipation as the lights dim to the satisfying crunch of popcorn, there is something magical about watching a film on the big screen. In Sarasota, Florida, you will find various cinemas, ranging from modern multiplexes with the latest technology to cozy independent theaters highlighting art-house and indie films. This thriving city offers movie buffs an unforgettable experience, whether you are searching for the latest Hollywood blockbuster or a thought-provoking documentary. So, grab a tub of popcorn, sit back, and let the cinematic adventures begin.

SARASOTA UNCOVERED

Regal Hollywood Stadium 11
1993 Main St, Sarasota, FL 34236
Phone: (941) 954-5768
www.regmovies.com

Description: These modern multiplex features eleven screens, showing the latest Hollywood blockbusters in a comfortable setting. Prices are in the $$ range, with plenty of food and beverage options.

Burns Court Cinema
506 Burns Ct, Sarasota, FL 34236
Phone: (941) 955-3456
www.filmsociety.org

Description: Burns Court Cinema is an intimate, independent theater run by the Sarasota Film Society. Highlighting indie, foreign, and documentary films, ticket prices are in the $$ range.

CinéBistro Siesta Key
3501 S Tamiami Trail, Sarasota, FL 34239
Phone: (941) 361-2456
www.cinebistro.com

Description: This luxury theater offers a sophisticated movie experience with in-theater dining and a full bar. With ticket prices in the $$$ range, it is perfect for a special night out.

AMC Sarasota 12
8201 S Tamiami Trail, Sarasota, FL 34238
Phone: (941) 922-3130
www.amctheatres.com

Description: AMC Sarasota 12 is a famous cinema featuring twelve screens, modern amenities, and the latest films. Prices are in the $$ range, with various concessions available.

Parkway 8 Cinemas
6300 N Lockwood Ridge Rd, Sarasota, FL 34243
Phone: (941) 360-6741
www.parkwaycinemas.com

Description: Parkway 8 Cinemas is a budget-friendly option, with ticket prices in the $ range. This local favorite offers a mix of recent releases and second-run movies.

Sarasota Film Festival
332 Cocoanut Ave, Sarasota, FL 34236
Phone: (941) 364-9514
www.sarasotafilmfestival.com

Description: The Sarasota Film Festival is an annual event highlighting the best in independent cinema, just a ticket for film enthusiasts.

Lakewood Ranch Cinemas
10715 Rodeo Dr, Lakewood Ranch, FL 34202
Phone: (941) 955-3456
www.filmsociety.org

Description: Operated by the Sarasota Film Society, this theater features six screens and various film genres. Prices are in the $$ range, and it is just a short drive from Sarasota.

Terrace 4 Cinemas
1131 N Tamiami Trail, Sarasota, FL 34236
Phone: (941) 358-2456
www.terracecinemas.com

Description: Terrace 4 Cinemas is a charming, small theater focusing on art-house and foreign films. Ticket prices are in the $$ range, and the theater is known for its welcoming atmosphere.

SARASOTA UNCOVERED

Fringe Film Festival
Various locations, Sarasota, FL
www.fringefilmfestival.org

Description: The Fringe Film Festival is an annual event highlighting experimental and avant-garde films worldwide. Ticket prices vary, but it is an excellent opportunity to explore cutting-edge cinema.

The Starlite Room
1001 Cocoanut Ave, Sarasota, FL 34236
Phone: (941) 312-0000
www.thestarliteroom.com

Description: The Starlite Room is a unique combination of a movie theater and a dining establishment, offering dinner and a movie in one location. Prices are in the $$$ range, making it a perfect spot for a special night out.

Chapter 18 / Museums

Sarasota, Florida, known for its vibrant arts scene, is a treasure trove of museums and cultural institutions. The museums in Sarasota are as diverse as the city itself, highlighting everything from world-class art and historical artifacts to quirky collections and interactive exhibits. Whether you are an art lover, a history buff, or simply looking for an educational and entertaining way to spend a day, Sarasota's museums offer something for everyone. As you stroll through the city, you will immerse yourself in a world of creativity and discovery that will inspire and enlighten you. In this guide, we will explore the top museums in Sarasota, Florida, so you can make the most of your visit to this cultural haven.

SARASOTA UNCOVERED

The Ringling
5401 Bay Shore Rd, Sarasota, FL 34243
Phone: (941) 359-5700
www.ringling.org

The Ringling is a magnificent and expansive cultural complex that combines art, history, and performance, making it a must-see destination in Sarasota. With admission fees in the $$ range, the estate offers a fascinating glimpse into the lives of circus magnate John Ringling and his wife, Mable. Visitors can explore the beautiful Ca' d'Zan Mansion, admire the vast art collection at the Museum of Art, and learn about the rich history of the circus at the Circus Museum. The property also features lush gardens and the historic Asolo Theater, highlighting live performances. The Ringling offers a diverse and engaging experience for the entire family, making it a top attraction in Sarasota.

Mike Avey

The Dali Museum
1 Dali Blvd, St. Petersburg, FL 33701
Phone: (727) 823-3767
www.thedali.org

Located just an hour's drive from Sarasota, The Dali Museum in St. Petersburg is a must-visit destination for art lovers. Housing the most extensive collection of Salvador Dali's work outside of Europe, this museum is a surrealistic wonderland that offers a unique and immersive experience. Explore the mind of the iconic Spanish artist through his paintings, drawings, sculptures, and photographs. With admission prices in the $$$ range, The Dali Museum is an unforgettable journey into the world of surrealism and a fantastic opportunity to delve into the creative genius of Salvador Dali. Do not miss the museum's stunning architecture, featuring a glass geodesic structure known as the "Enigma" and a labyrinthine garden that reflects Dali's artistic vision. Whether you long-time admirer of Dali's work or new to his captivating universe, visiting The Dali Museum will surely inspire and amaze you.

SARASOTA UNCOVERED

Mote Marine Laboratory & Aquarium
1600 Ken Thompson Pkwy, Sarasota, FL 34236
Phone: (941) 388-4441
www.mote.org

The Mote Marine Laboratory & Aquarium is a world-renowned marine research institution that offers an interactive and educational experience for visitors of all ages. With admission prices in the $$ range, Mote Aquarium allows guests to discover the ocean's wonders through up-close encounters with diverse marine life, including sharks, sea turtles, manatees, and more. Enjoy interactive exhibits, learn about cutting-edge research, and witness the dedicated efforts of the Mote staff in the care and conservation of marine species. A visit to Mote Marine Laboratory & Aquarium is a memorable and inspiring way to immerse yourself in the captivating world of marine life.

Marie Selby Botanical Gardens
1534 Mound St, Sarasota, FL 34236
Phone: (941) 366-5731
www.selby.org

The Marie Selby Botanical Gardens is a tranquil oasis in the heart of Sarasota, highlighting a diverse array of tropical plants and breathtaking landscapes. With admission fees in the $$ range, visitors can explore the enchanting gardens, which feature the world's most extensive epiphytes, including orchids and bromeliads. Stroll along the winding pathways, admire the lush foliage, and discover the fascinating world of plant research and conservation at the on-site laboratory. The gardens also host various events, such as art exhibitions, concerts, and educational programs, making Marie Selby Botanical Gardens a vibrant and captivating destination for nature lovers and families.

Marietta Museum of Art & Whimsy
2121 N Tamiami Trail, Sarasota, FL 34234
Phone: (941) 364-3399
www.mariettamuseum.org

This charming museum highlights an eclectic collection of art and whimsical objects. With free admission, the Marietta Museum of Art & Whimsy is a must-visit for those who appreciate the quirky and unusual.

Sarasota Classic Car Museum
5500 N Tamiami Trail, Sarasota, FL 34243
Phone: (941) 355-6228
www.sarasotacarmuseum.org

Description: Automobile enthusiasts will love the Sarasota Classic Car Museum, which houses an impressive collection of vintage and rare vehicles. With admission prices in the $ range, this museum is an excellent stop for car lovers.

South Florida Museum
201 10th St W, Bradenton, FL 34205
Phone: (941) 746-4131
www.southfloridamuseum.org

This museum, located in nearby Bradenton, features an exhibit on the natural and cultural history of the region, as well as a planetarium and an aquarium. With admission prices in the $$ range, the South Florida Museum is perfect for an educational day trip.

Art Center Sarasota
707 N Tamiami Trail, Sarasota, FL 34236
Phone: (941) 365-2032
www.artsarasota.org

Art Center Sarasota is a dynamic art center featuring rotating exhibitions, classes, and workshops for all ages. With free admission, this museum is a great spot for art lovers and creatives.

SARASOTA UNCOVERED

Sarasota County History Center
701 N Tamiami Trail, Sarasota, FL 34236
Phone: (941) 861-5000
www.scgov.net/history

This historical center highlights the rich history of Sarasota County through engaging exhibits and events. With free admission, the Sarasota County History Center is an excellent resource for those interested in local history.

The Powel Crosley Estate
8374 N Tamiami Trail, Sarasota, FL 34243
Phone: (941) 722-3244
www.powelcrosleyestate.com

Description: The Powel Crosley Estate is a stunning historic mansion that offers guided tours and hosts special events. With admission prices in the $ range, this beautiful estate offers a glimpse into Sarasota's past.

Sarasota Military Academy Museum
801 N Orange Ave, Sarasota, FL 34236
Phone: (941) 926-1700
www.sarasotamilitaryacademy.org

Description: This museum at the Sarasota Military Academy highlights military memorabilia and artifacts. With free admission, the Sarasota Military Academy Museum is perfect for those interested in military history.

Chapter 19 /
Spa, Yoga, Meditation

Sarasota, Florida, a picturesque coastal city, is a haven for those seeking relaxation, rejuvenation, and inner peace. Whether you are a busy professional, a tourist eager to unwind, or a local needing a little self-care, Sarasota offers an abundance of luxurious spas, tranquil yoga studios, and serene meditation spaces. These oases of calm provide a welcome escape from the stresses of daily life, allowing visitors to recharge their minds, bodies, and souls. In this bustling paradise, indulge in soothing spa treatments, deepen your yoga practice, and discover the transformative power of meditation. So, take a deep breath, let go of your worries, and embark on a journey of healing and self-discovery in the beautiful Sarasota.

SARASOTA UNCOVERED

The Spa at The Ritz-Carlton
1111 Ritz Carlton Dr, Sarasota, FL 34236
Phone: (941) 309-2090   www.ritzcarlton.com

The Spa at The Ritz-Carlton, Sarasota, is a luxurious retreat that offers a wide range of pampering treatments and services in a tranquil and elegant setting. With prices in the $$$ range, this upscale spa epitomizes relaxation and rejuvenation.

Shore Rejuvenation Day Spa
1092 S. Tamiami Trail, Sarasota, FL 34236
Phone: (941) 312-4402   www.shorerejuvenation.com

Shore Rejuvenation Day Spa is a boutique spa offering various personalized treatments to enhance your well-being. With prices in the $$ range, experience the restorative power of massage, facials, and body treatments in a serene and intimate setting.

Pineapple Yoga + Cycling Studio
517 S Pineapple Ave, Sarasota, FL 34236
Phone: (941) 210-3739   www.pineappleyogastudio.net

Pineapple Yoga + Cycling Studio provides a welcoming environment for yogis of all levels. With prices in the $ range, choose from various classes, including vinyasa, yin, and restorative yoga, as well as stimulating indoor cycling sessions.

CircuSoul Yoga
4141 S Tamiami Trail #6, Sarasota, FL 34231
Phone: (941) 922-9642   www.circusoul.com

CircuSoul Yoga is a unique studio that offers traditional yoga classes, aerial yoga, and circus arts. With prices in the $ range, explore new ways to challenge your body, mind, and spirit in a playful and supportive atmosphere.

The Met Fashion House Day Spa & Salon
35 S Blvd of the Presidents, Sarasota, FL 34236
Phone: (941) 388-3991   www.themetsarasota.com

Description: The Met is a luxurious day spa and salon offering a wide range of beauty and wellness services. With prices in the $$ range, treat yourself to a relaxing massage, a revitalizing facial, or a stylish haircut in an opulent and soothing setting.

Sarasota Mindfulness Institute
1530 Dolphin St, Sarasota, FL 34236
Phone: (941) 350-7992
www.sarasotamindfulness.org

Sarasota Mindfulness Institute is dedicated to fostering mindfulness and meditation practices. With prices in the $ range, attend workshops, group sessions, and classes to cultivate inner peace and self-awareness in a supportive and serene environment.

L. Spa
556 S Pineapple Ave, Sarasota, FL 34236
Phone: (941) 906-1358   www.lspa.life

L. Spa is a cozy, boutique-style day spa offering various relaxing and rejuvenating treatments. With prices in the $$ range, indulge in customized facials, therapeutic massages, and soothing body treatments designed to help you feel and look your best.

Garden of the Heart Yoga Center
2888 Ringling Blvd, Sarasota, FL 34237
Phone: (941) 341-9781 www.gardenoftheheartyoga.com

Garden of the Heart Yoga Center is a warm and inviting yoga studio that offers classes for all levels. With prices in the $ range, choose from various yoga styles, including Hatha, Yin, and Vinyasa, to strengthen your body, calm your mind, and nourish your spirit.

SARASOTA UNCOVERED

Essence Mind Body Studio
3403 Magic Oak Ln, Sarasota, FL 34232
Phone: (941) 356-1989
www.essencemindbodystudio.com

Description: Essence Mind Body Studio is a tranquil space dedicated to holistic wellness. With prices in the $ range, participate in yoga classes, guided meditation sessions, and healing workshops to restore balance and harmony to your mind, body, and soul.

Ocean Love Ayurveda & Massage
1341 Main St, Sarasota, FL 34236
Phone: (941) 320-7803
www.oceanloveayurveda.com

Description: Ocean Love Ayurveda & Massage offers a unique healing experience through the ancient wisdom of Ayurveda. With prices in the $$ range, enjoy rejuvenating Ayurvedic treatments, personalized consultations, and therapeutic massage to restore balance and vitality.

Chapter 20 /
Theater Performances

Sarasota, Florida, a beautiful haven nestled along the Gulf Coast, is renowned for its alluring white sandy beaches, clear waters, and lush tropical landscapes. However, this picturesque destination offers more than just natural beauty; it is a thriving epicenter of arts and culture, boasting an impressive array of performance theaters highlighting the finest dramatic and musical talent. Sarasota's performance theaters are deeply ingrained in the city's identity, offering locals and visitors alike a wide variety of entertainment options that span from classic plays to contemporary productions, as well as mesmerizing musicals and awe-inspiring dance performances. Allow yourself to be transported to another world as you embark on a captivating journey through Sarasota's enchanting performance theaters. Stories come to life, creativity flourishes, and unforgettable memories are made.

SARASOTA UNCOVERED

Asolo Repertory Theatre
5555 N Tamiami Trail, Sarasota, FL 34243
Phone: (941) 351-8000   www.asolorep.org

Asolo Repertory Theatre, a premier regional theater in Sarasota, is renowned for its diverse productions, from classic plays to cutting-edge contemporary works. The theater's commitment to producing the highest caliber of performances has made it an integral part of the Sarasota arts scene. With ticket prices in the $$$ range, experience amazing theatrical shows in an intimate, state-of-the-art setting and be captivated by the talent and creativity on display.

Van Wezel Performing Arts Hall
777 N Tamiami Trail, Sarasota, FL 34236
Phone: (941) 263-6799   www.vanwezel.org

Van Wezel Performing Arts Hall is a stunning architectural masterpiece hosting various world-class performances. Designed by the renowned architect Frank Lloyd Wright's firm, this iconic venue boasts an eye-catching exterior and an impressive lineup of shows. With ticket prices in the $$-$$$ range, immerse yourself in breathtaking performances that range from Broadway musicals and top-notch comedians to renowned orchestras and ballet companies.

Florida Studio Theatre
1241 N Palm Ave, Sarasota, FL 34236
Phone: (941) 366-9000   www.floridastudiotheatre.org

Description: Florida Studio Theatre is a bustling cultural hub that offers a rich lineup of contemporary plays, musicals, and comedies. Known for producing new and thought-provoking works, this vibrant venue invites audiences to engage in stimulating conversations nd explore new perspectives. With ticket prices in the $$ range, Florida Studio Theatre promises a unique, entertaining experience that will leave you both moved and inspired.

Sarasota Opera House
61 N Pineapple Ave, Sarasota, FL 34236
Phone: (941) 328-1300   www.sarasotaopera.org

Description: Sarasota Opera House is a beautifully restored historic venue that celebrates the art of opera. Initially built in 1926, this magnificent building has been lovingly restored and modernized, preserving its historic charm. With ticket prices in the $$$ range, indulge in world-class performances of classic and lesser-known operas, special events, and concerts in this intimate and acoustically superb setting.

The Players Centre for Performing Arts
838 N Tamiami Trail, Sarasota, FL 34236
Phone: (941) 365-2494   www.theplayers.org

Description: The Players Centre for Performing Arts is a community-driven theater highlighting diverse productions, from classic plays to original works. This lively venue fosters local talent and encourages creativity, offering engaging performances that reflect the spirit of the community. With ticket prices in the $-$$ range, support local artists and enjoy a captivating night out at the theater that will leave a lasting impression on your heart and mind.

SARASOTA UNCOVERED

Chapter 21 /
Malls and Shopping

Ah, shopping — the universal pleasure that transcends borders and cultures. In Sarasota, Florida, the shopping experience is elevated to an art form, thanks to the city's diverse array of malls and shopping centers. Whether you are searching for designer clothes or unique gifts or want to indulge in retail therapy, Sarasota's shopping centers will surely delight and inspire you. Sarasota's retail landscape is as vibrant and diverse as the city, from upscale boutiques and luxury stores to open-air markets and charming local shops. Immerse yourself in fashion, art, and culture as you explore Sarasota, Florida's best malls and shopping centers. So, grab your wallet and put on your most comfortable shoes because we are about to embark on a fabulous shopping adventure!

The Mall at University Town Center
140 University Town Center Dr, Sarasota, FL 34243
Phone: (941) 552-7000
www.mallatutc.com

The Mall at University Town Center is a premier shopping destination in Sarasota, boasting over one hundred upscale shops, department stores, and dining options. With a wide range of stores from $$$ to $$$$, you will find something for everyone at this stylish and modern shopping center.

St. Armands Circle
300 Madison Dr, Sarasota, FL 34236
Phone: (941) 388-1554
www.starmandscircleassoc.com

St. Armands Circle is a charming outdoor shopping and dining destination that offers a unique, European-inspired atmosphere. Featuring over 130 shops and restaurants ranging from $$ to $$$$, this picturesque shopping area is perfect for a leisurely day of browsing and indulging.

Siesta Key Village
5124 Ocean Blvd, Sarasota, FL 34242
www.siestakeyvillage.com

Siesta Key Village is a laid-back, beachy shopping district with boutique shops, art galleries, and casual eateries. With prices in the $$ to $$$ range, it is the perfect spot for finding unique gifts, beachwear, and local treasures.

Westfield Sarasota Square
8201 S Tamiami Trail, Sarasota, FL 34238
Phone: (941) 922-9609

Westfield Sarasota Square is a classic shopping mall with many stores, restaurants, and entertainment options. Catering to a range of budgets from $ to $$$, this mall offers a convenient and enjoyable shopping experience for the whole family.

SARASOTA UNCOVERED

Chapter 22 /
Farmer Markets

There is something undeniably magical about strolling through a bustling farmers market on a sun-drenched day, with the air permeated by fresh produce, the aroma of artisanal bread, and the lively chatter of friendly vendors. Sarasota, Florida, is a haven for those who appreciate local farmers markets' charm, authenticity, and vibrant atmosphere. These markets offer more than just a delightful shopping experience; they also nurture and support local farmers, artisans, and small businesses, creating a sense of community that cannot be replicated within the sterile confines of a supermarket.

As you meander through the colorful aisles of Sarasota's farmer's markets, you will be greeted by rainbow-hued fruits and vegetables, their enticing flavors promising culinary delights. The air is filled with the tantalizing aroma of freshly baked bread and pastries, tempting you to indulge in their golden, flaky goodness. As you explore further, you will discover an array of specialty products, from local honey and homemade jams to handcrafted cheeses and artisanal chocolates, each embodying the passion and dedication of the individuals who crafted them.

Sarasota's farmer's markets are more than just a paradise for foodies seeking the freshest, most flavorful ingredients; they are treasure troves for those searching for unique, handcrafted items. As you wander among the stalls, you will encounter skilled artisans highlighting their wares, from one-of-a-kind jewelry and pottery to handmade soaps and textiles. Each item tells a story, reflecting the heart and soul of the creator and offering a tangible connection to the vibrant culture of Sarasota.

Beyond the delectable foods and exquisite crafts, Sarasota's farmer's markets also serve as lively social hubs where you can connect with locals, learn about the region's rich history and traditions, and catch live music. The atmosphere is warm and welcoming as vendors and shoppers share their stories, swap recipes, and revel in the simple joys of community connection.

SARASOTA UNCOVERED

Whether you are an ardent foodie on the hunt for the freshest, most delicious ingredients, a treasure hunter seeking out unique, handcrafted items, or simply someone who appreciates the joy and camaraderie of a bustling market, Sarasota's farmer's markets are sure to enchant you. As you wander through these vibrant, lively spaces, you will be immersed in a world of sensory delights, where Sarasota's sights, sounds, and flavors come together to create an unforgettable experience that will linger in your heart and soul long after you have left the market behind.

Sarasota Farmers Market
1 N Lemon Ave, Sarasota, FL 34236
Phone: (941) 225-9256
sarasotafarmersmarket.org

Description: The Sarasota Farmers Market is a beloved institution in downtown Sarasota, with a fantastic selection of fresh produce, artisanal goods, and delicious prepared foods. With prices in the $ to $$ range, this bustling market is an ideal destination for shoppers of all budgets.

Phillippi Farmhouse Market
5500 S Tamiami Trail, Sarasota, FL 34231
Phone: (941) 861-5000
farmhousemarket.org

Description: Set in the picturesque Phillippi Estate Park, the Phillippi Farmhouse Market offers a delightful mix of fresh produce, locally made goods, and delicious food trucks. With its $ to $$ price range, this market is a must-visit for those seeking a relaxed and scenic shopping experience.

Central Sarasota Farmers Market
4454 Beneva Rd, Sarasota, FL 34233
centralsarasotafarmersmarket.com

Description: The Central Sarasota Farmers Market is a community-driven market emphasizing sustainability and supporting local farmers and artisans. Featuring various goods at prices from this market is perfect for those looking to shop local and enjoy a friendly atmosphere.

Siesta Key Farmers Market
5104 Ocean Blvd, Siesta Key, FL 34242
siestakeyfarmersmarket.org

Description: Nestled in the heart of Siesta Key Village, the Siesta Key Farmers Market boasts a diverse array of products, from fresh produce to handmade crafts, with prices ranging from $ to $$$. This charming market is an excellent stop for visitors exploring the beautiful Siesta Key area.

Venice Farmers Market
401 W Venice Ave, Venice, FL 34285
Phone: (941) 445-9209
thevenicefarmersmarket.org

Just a short drive from Sarasota, the Venice Farmers Market offers a delightful shopping experience by the sea. With reasonable prices, shoppers can find fresh produce, local crafts, and tasty treats while enjoying the ocean breeze.

Closing Summary

SARASOTA UNCOVERED
Chapter 23 / Art Galleries

Art has the power to inspire, provoke thought, and evoke emotions. Sarasota, Florida, has a thriving art scene that reflects the city's rich cultural history and diverse creative influences. Sarasota's art galleries highlight an impressive range of styles, mediums, and genres, from internationally renowned artists to emerging local talent. As you explore the city's captivating art scene, you will encounter a vibrant tapestry of artistic expression that resonates with the area's unique character and charm.

Whether you are an avid collector looking to add a new piece to your collection, an aspiring artist seeking inspiration, or simply a curious traveler who appreciates the beauty of artistic creations, Sarasota's art galleries offer a feast for the eyes and the soul. As you meander through these gallery spaces, you will be immersed in a world of creative expression, where bold strokes and delicate details come together to tell a story that transcends time and place. This enchanting journey through Sarasota's art scene will leave a lasting impression on your heart as you discover the wonders of creativity and the power of human imagination.

Allyn Gallup Contemporary Art - $$
1288 N Palm Ave, Sarasota, FL 34236
(941) 366-2454 allyngallup.com

This gallery features a thoughtfully curated selection of contemporary art by established and emerging artists, offering a visually engaging experience that challenges the viewer's perspective.

Art Center Sarasota - $$
707 N Tamiami Trail, Sarasota, FL 34236
(941) 365-2032 artsarasota.org

Home to various exhibitions, Art Center Sarasota, highlights local, regional, and national artists, providing a platform for creative expression and community engagement.

Dabbert Gallery - $$$
76 S Palm Ave, Sarasota, FL 34236
(941) 955-1315 dabbertgallery.com

Specializing in contemporary fine art, Dabbert Gallery presents an eclectic mix of paintings, sculptures, and photographs by internationally recognized artists.

Galleria Silecchia - $$$$
20 S Palm Ave, Sarasota, FL 34236
(941) 365-7414 galleriasilecchia.com

Highlighting a diverse range of contemporary and traditional art, Galleria Silecchia offers an inspiring collection of works from renowned artists around the globe.

SARASOTA UNCOVERED

.M. Chapel Projects - $$
2087 Princeton St, Sarasota, FL 34237
(941) 374-3492 mchapelprojects.com

This innovative gallery space hosts engaging exhibitions and installations, promoting the exploration of contemporary art and fostering creative dialogue.

McIntosh Art Gallery - $$
1833 Morrill St, Sarasota, FL 34236
(941) 951-2100 mcintoshartgallery.com

Featuring an extensive collection of fine art and sculpture, McIntosh Art Gallery offers a visually stimulating experience for collectors and enthusiasts alike.

Nancy Markoe Gallery - $$
2121 Main St #100, Sarasota, FL 34237
(941) 260-9159 nancymarkoegallery.com

Located in the heart of Sarasota, Nancy Markoe Gallery highlights a wide array of artworks by established and emerging artists, focusing on American contemporary art.

Paradise Gallery - $$$
610 Central Ave, Sarasota, FL 34236
(941) 366-7155 paradisegalleryart.com

With a mission to bring joy through art, Paradise Gallery offers a diverse collection of works, including paintings, glass art, and sculptures, representing various styles and techniques.

State of the Arts Gallery - $$$
1525 State St, Sarasota, FL 34236
(941) 955-2787   stateoftheartsgallery.com

This contemporary fine art gallery highlights a wide range of artists, offering an eclectic mix of styles, mediums, and subject matter that reflects the vibrant spirit of Sarasota's art scene.

The Celery Barn Gallery - $$
266 S Links Ave, Sarasota, FL 34236
(941) 321-7799   thecelerybarn.com

Housed in a charmingly restored historic building, The Celery Barn Gallery presents a unique and intimate setting for experiencing the works of local and regional artists.

SARASOTA UNCOVERED

Chapter 24 /
Independent coffee cafes

Sarasota, Florida, the beautiful Gulf Coast gem, offers stunning beaches, a rich cultural scene, and a thriving independent coffee café culture. For those who crave their daily caffeine fix or seek a cozy spot to relax and catch up with friends, Sarasota's coffee scene is like a warm, aromatic hug that invites you in and keeps you coming back for more. As you wander through the city, you will discover charming coffee shops with character and personality, each offering its unique blend of flavors, ambiance, and hospitality.

In these indie coffee havens, enthusiastic baristas treat coffee-making as an art, carefully selecting beans, perfecting the brewing process, and crafting each cup with love and attention. As you sip on your handcrafted latte or aromatic pour-over, you will feel the dedication that goes into every drop. The delightful pastries, light bites, and sandwiches available at many of these cafés are the perfect accompaniments to your beverage, satisfying both your taste buds and your appetite.

Perq Coffee Bar - $$
1821 Hillview St, Sarasota, FL 34239
Phone: (941) 955-8101   www.perqcoffeebar.com

Perq Coffee Bar is a modern, hip café focusing on single-origin beans and artisanal brewing methods. Their cozy atmosphere and knowledgeable staff make it a must-visit spot for coffee connoisseurs.

The Clever Cup - $
6530 Gateway Ave, Sarasota, FL 34231
Phone: (941) 281-2662   www.theclevercup.com

The Clever Cup is a quaint, eclectic café that offers various locally roasted coffee and homemade pastries. The warm, inviting atmosphere makes it an ideal place to unwind and catch up with friends.

Buddy Brew Coffee - $$
1289 N Palm Ave, Sarasota, FL 34236
Phone: (941) 374-7186   www.buddybrew.com

Buddy Brew Coffee is a trendy, industrial-chic café that serves expertly crafted coffee drinks and delicious baked goods. Their passion for coffee and community shines through every cup.

Kahwa Coffee - $$
1487 2nd St, Sarasota, FL 34236
Phone: (941) 220-4301   www.kahwacoffee.com

Kahwa Coffee is a bright, modern café focusing on high-quality, ethically sourced beans. The friendly staff and delectable menu make it a popular spot for a caffeine boost.

SARASOTA UNCOVERED

Pastry Art - $$
1512 Main St, Sarasota, FL 34236
Phone: (941) 955-7545   www.pastryartbakerycafe.com
Pastry Art is a cozy café offering brewed coffee drinks and mouthwatering pastries expertly. The welcoming atmosphere and central location make it an excellent leisure break spot.

Out and About Coffee - $
2241 Ringling Blvd, Sarasota, FL 34237
Phone: (941) 726-8150   www.outandaboutcoffee.com
Out and About Coffee is a unique mobile coffee shop that brings delicious espresso drinks and friendly service to the community. Their dedication to quality and sustainability sets them apart.

C'est La Vie! - $$$
1553 Main St, Sarasota, FL 34236
Phone: (941) 906-9575
www.cestlaviesarasota.com
C'est La Vie! is a charming French bistro and coffee shop offering an authentic European café experience. Indulge in their exquisite pastries and expertly crafted coffee drinks while enjoying the Parisian ambiance.

The Reserve - $$
1322 N Tamiami Trail, Sarasota, FL 34236
Phone: (941) 702-5859
www.thereservesrq.com
The Reserve is a rustic, cozy café, bookstore, and event space that combines excellent coffee with a passion for literature and community. Sip on a latte while browsing their extensive book collection.

Lelu Coffee Lounge - $$
5251 Ocean Blvd, Siesta Key, Sarasota, FL 34242
Phone: (941) 346-5358   www.lelucoffee.com

Lelu Coffee Lounge is a vibrant, beachy café found on Siesta Key. Enjoy expertly crafted coffee drinks, delicious bites, and live music in a fun and relaxed atmosphere.

Green Bean Coffee House - $
501 N Beneva Rd #510, Sarasota, FL 34232
Phone: (941) 952-9975
www.greenbeancoffeehouse.business.site

Green Bean Coffee House is a cozy, homey café offering various coffee drinks and homemade treats. The welcoming atmosphere makes it a perfect spot to relax with friends or do some work.

Café in the Park - $
2010 Adams Ln, Sarasota, FL 34237
Phone: (941) 361-3032
www.cafeintheparksarasota.com

Café in the Park is a charming outdoor café in Payne Park, offering various coffee drinks, sandwiches, and live music. Enjoy the beautiful park setting as you sip your favorite brew.

Café L'Europe - $$$$
431 St Armands Cir, Sarasota, FL 34236
Phone: (941) 388-4415   www.cafeleurope.net

Café L'Europe is an elegant European-style café that offers a luxurious coffee experience. Indulge in their exceptional coffee drinks, fine pastries, and sophisticated atmosphere.

SARASOTA UNCOVERED

Black Gold Coffee Roasters - $$
2385 E Venice Ave, Venice, FL 34292
Phone: (941) 488-8242
(www.blackgoldcoffeeroasters.com)*

Black Gold Coffee Roasters is a specialty coffee shop that roasts its beans in-house, ensuring a fresh and flavorful cup of coffee. Their passion for quality and sustainability is evident in every sip.

Sift Bakehouse - $$
1383 McAnsh Square, Sarasota, FL 34236
Phone: (941) 203-8528   www.siftbakehouse.com

Sift Bakehouse is a delightful bakery and coffee shop offering an array of delicious pastries and expertly crafted coffee drinks. The charming atmosphere makes it a perfect place to enjoy a sweet treat and a cup of joe.

Origin Craft Beer & Coffee Bar - $$
1837 Hillview St, Sarasota, FL 34239
Phone: (941) 316-9222   www.origincraftbeer.com

Origin Craft Beer & Coffee Bar is a unique establishment that combines a love for craft beer and specialty coffee. The cozy, inviting atmosphere is great for relaxing with friends and enjoying a drink.

Chapter 25 / Restaurants

Sarasota area, a culinary haven that promises a delightful and diverse gastronomic experience for food lovers of all kinds. With its unique blend of cultures and influences, Sarasota's dining scene boasts various flavors, from fresh seafood caught in the Gulf of Mexico to the finest international cuisine. As you explore this enchanting city, you will soon discover that the restaurants here are as varied as those who call Sarasota home.

One of the highlights of dining in Greater Sarasota is the opportunity to indulge in the freshest seafood, often served with a Floridian twist. From casual beachside eateries to upscale waterfront dining, there is no shortage of establishments offering mouthwatering seafood dishes, including succulent shrimp, tender grouper, and the ever-popular stone crab. And for those craving a taste of the exotic, Sarasota's culinary scene also features an impressive

SARASOTA UNCOVERED

selection of international restaurants, ranging from authentic Italian trattorias and aromatic Indian curries to delectable sushi and Latin-inspired tapas.

No visit to Sarasota would be complete without exploring its unique dining experiences that will leave a lasting impression.

Whether It is a farm-to-table cafe highlighting the best local produce or a hidden gem tucked away in one of the city's charming neighborhoods, there is something for everyone in this culinary paradise. As you embark on your gastronomic adventure through Greater Sarasota, you will be treated to incredible flavors but also experience the warm hospitality and welcoming atmosphere the city is known for. So, prepare your taste buds for an unforgettable journey through the diverse and delicious world of Sarasota dining.

Indigenous ($$$)
239 S Links Ave, Sarasota, FL 34236,
Phone: (941) 706-4740
www.indigenousrestaurant.com/

Indigenous showcases Chef Steve Phelps' commitment to sustainable, local, and seasonal ingredients in a beautifully restored historic cottage. Diners can relish the warm and inviting atmosphere while savoring thoughtfully crafted dishes like wild boar pappardelle, crispy fish collar, or the famous snapper throats.

Selva Grill ($$$)
1345 Main St, Sarasota, FL 34236,
Phone: (941) 362-4427 www.selvagrill.com/

At Selva Grill, guests can expect a rich and stylish dining experience that combines Latin and Peruvian flavors. The menu offers extensive ceviches, tiraditos, and imaginative entrees, such as the Churrasco a la Selva, all with artistic flair. The chic, urban ambiance sets the perfect stage for a memorable dining experience.

Owen's Fish Camp ($$)
516 Burns Ln, Sarasota, FL 34236,
Phone: (941) 951-6936
www.owensfishcamp.com/

Embracing the charm of Old Florida, Owen's Fish Camp serves southern-style seafood dishes in a laid-back, rustic setting adorned with fishing memorabilia. The menu features comfort food favorites like the Low Country Boil, Fried Green Tomato BLT, and daily specials highlighting the freshest catch. The outdoor area, with live music and a tire swing, adds to the nostalgia.

Sardinia ($$$)
5770 S Tamiami Trail, Sarasota, FL 34231,
Phone: (941) 702-9297
www.sardiniasrq.com/

At Sardinia, guests are transported to the heart of Italy with a menu that highlights the distinctive flavors of the island of Sardinia. The warm, rustic decor sets the stage for enjoying wood-fired pizzas, homemade pasta dishes, and an impressive wine list. The Fregola con Arselle, a traditional Sardinian dish featuring clams and fregola pasta, is a must-try.

SARASOTA UNCOVERED

Shore ($$$)
465 John Ringling Blvd, Sarasota, FL 34236,
Phone: (941) 296-0301   www.dineshore.com/

Shore brings a touch of retro-chic style to Sarasota's dining scene with its mid-century-inspired design and stunning views of Sarasota Bay. The menu features American classics with a contemporary twist, such as the Shore Burger, made with wagyu beef and bacon jam, or the indulgent Lobster Pot Pie. Their craft cocktails are the perfect accompaniment to any meal.

State Street Eating House + Cocktails ($$$)
465 John Ringling Blvd, Sarasota, FL 34236,
Phone: (941) 296-0301   www.dineshore.com/

State Street Eating House + Cocktails is a hip and welcoming spot that offers an elevated American dining experience. The menu boasts dishes like the succulent short rib stroganoff and local catch of the day, all prepared with exceptional diligence. The dimly lit, stylish atmosphere is the perfect setting to enjoy one of their inventive craft cocktails.

Michael's On East ($$$$)
1212 East Ave S, Sarasota, FL 34239,
Phone: (941) 366-0007   www.bestfood.com/

This Sarasota icon has been serving award-winning cuisine for over 30 years. Michael's On East offers a fine dining experience featuring innovative, globally inspired dishes like the Chilean Sea Bass and the Colorado Rack of Lamb. The elegant, sophisticated atmosphere and impeccable service make it a favorite for special occasions or a memorable night out.

Yume Sushi ($$$)
1532 Main St, Sarasota, FL 34236
Phone: (941) 363-0604   www.yumesushisarasota.com/

Yume Sushi is a modern Japanese gem where the culinary team creates artful and innovative sushi and sashimi presentations. Alongside their sushi offerings, the menu also features Japanese classics such as ramen and tempura and a delightful selection of sake and cocktails. The contemporary, minimalist decor provides a serene backdrop for an exceptional dining experience.

Antoine's Restaurant ($$$)
1100 N Tuttle Ave, Sarasota, FL 34237,
Phone: (941) 331-1400
www.antoinesrestaurant.com/

Experience the best French and Belgian cuisine at Antoine's, where the menu features a delightful blend of European flavors. Signature dishes like the mussels cooked in various sauces, delicious duck confit, and the indulgent chocolate lava cake make this a dining experience you will not forget. The cozy, intimate atmosphere only adds to the charm of this hidden gem.

Duval's Fresh. Local. Seafood. ($$$)
1435 Main St, Sarasota, FL 34236,
Phone: (941) 312-4001   www.duvalsfls.com/

At Duval's, you will enjoy an upscale seafood dining experience emphasizing fresh, locally sourced ingredients. Their menu highlights pan-seared scallops with sweet corn risotto, crab-crusted grouper with lobster, and various raw bar options. The stylish, contemporary decor and friendly service make Duval's a must-visit spot for seafood lovers.

SARASOTA UNCOVERED

El Toro Bravo ($$)
2720 Stickney Point Rd, Sarasota, FL 34231,
Phone: (941) 924-0006   www.eltorobravosarasota.com/

El Toro Bravo offers a taste of authentic Mexican cuisine in a vibrant and welcoming environment. With mouthwatering tacos, sizzling fajitas, and refreshing margaritas, you will feel like you have been transported south of the border. The festive atmosphere, colorful decor, and friendly service make it an ideal spot for a lively night out with friends or family.

Napule Ristorante Italian ($$$)
7129 S Tamiami Trail, Sarasota, FL 34231,
Phone: (941) 556-9639   www.napulerestaurant.com/

Step into the world of southern Italian cuisine at Napule, where dishes are inspired by the Amalfi Coast's rich culinary traditions. Every bite is a true delight, from the handmade pasta to the fresh seafood and tender veal dishes. The warm, inviting atmosphere and attentive service make you feel like dining in a cozy Italian trattoria.

Mediterraneo ($$$)
1970 Main St, Sarasota, FL 34236,
Phone: (941) 365-4122   www.mediterraneorest.com/

Mediterraneo brings the flavors of the Mediterranean to Sarasota with a menu that focuses on Italian classics and wood-fired pizzas. Signature dishes like the risotto with porcini mushrooms and the branzino with lemon-caper sauce are sure to please. The stylish, modern decor and impeccable service make Mediterraneo a popular choice for a memorable dining experience.

The Table Creekside ($$$$)
5365 S Tamiami Trail, Sarasota, FL 34231,
Phone: (941) 921-9465   www.tablesrq.com/

With stunning waterfront views and a menu that highlights fresh, globally inspired flavors, The Table Creekside offers an unparalleled dining experience. The diverse menu features dishes such as the Peruvian-style ceviche, the Thai bouillabaisse, and the mouthwatering filet mignon. The chic, romantic ambiance and outstanding service make this the perfect spot for a special occasion or a night to remember.

SARASOTA UNCOVERED

Chapter 26 / Quick Eating

Sarasota's quick-eating restaurant culture is as diverse and vibrant as its fine dining scene. In this sunny Florida city, you will find a tempting array of casual dining options catering to locals and visitors looking for delicious, convenient meals without compromising quality. From bustling food trucks to cozy cafes and everything in between, Sarasota's casual dining establishments are a testament to the city's love for delicious, no-fuss food perfect for on-the-go eating or a relaxed meal with friends.
.

Here are quick-eating restaurants in Sarasota, Florida, offering a range of culinary delights to satisfy every craving:

Nancy's Bar-B-Q ($$)
301 S Pineapple Ave, Sarasota, FL 34236,
Phone: (941) 366-2271   www.nancysbarbq.com/

Nancy's Bar-B-Q is a local favorite known for its mouthwatering smoked meats and Southern-style sides. With tender pulled pork, juicy brisket, and finger-licking ribs, there is something for every BBQ lover to enjoy.

Star Fish Company Market & Restaurant ($)
12306 46th Ave W, Cortez, FL 34215, Phone: (941) 794-1243   www.starfishcompany.com/

Located on the water, Star Fish Company offers fresh seafood dishes and breathtaking views. Feast on their famous grouper sandwich or indulge in the shrimp and grits while soaking in the laid-back, Old Florida atmosphere.

Selva Grill ($$$)
1345 Main St, Sarasota, FL 34236,
Phone: (941) 362-4427   www.selvagrill.com/

Selva Grill's Latin-inspired menu includes delectable tapas, ceviches, and entrees perfect for a quick bite or a leisurely meal. The stylish setting and creative dishes make for a memorable dining experience.

Mandeville Beer Garden ($$)
428 N Lemon Ave, Sarasota, FL 34236,
Phone: (941) 954-8688
www.mandevillebeergarden.com/

This lively outdoor beer garden offers an extensive selection of craft beers and delicious pub fares like burgers, sausages, and shareable appetizers. The relaxed atmosphere and frequent live music make it a great place to unwind with friends.

SARASOTA UNCOVERED

Smacks Burgers & Shakes ($)
2407 Bee Ridge Rd, Sarasota, FL 34239,
Phone: (941) 922-7673   www.smacksburgers.com/

Smacks is the go-to spot for juicy burgers, hand-cut fries, and creamy frozen custard. Their commitment to quality ingredients and a fun, retro atmosphere makes it a hit for locals and visitors.

Yoder's Amish Village ($$)
3434 Bahia Vista St, Sarasota, FL 34239,
Phone: (941) 955-7771   www.yodersrestaurant.com/

Known for its homemade pies and comfort food, Yoder's Amish Village serves hearty breakfasts, lunches, and dinners that make you feel right at home. Do not miss their famous fried chicken and delicious desserts.

Solorzano Bros. Pizzeria ($$)
215 Avenida Madera, Sarasota, FL 34242,
Phone: (941) 349-2767   www.solorzanobros.com/

Solorzano Bros. serves up authentic, thin-crust New York-style pizza, perfect for a quick, satisfying meal. Grab a slice or indulge in a pie loaded with your favorite toppings.

The Overton ($$)
1420 Blvd of the Arts, Sarasota, FL 34236,
Phone: (941) 500-9175   www.theovertonsrq.com/

The Overton is a trendy spot offering gourmet sandwiches, salads, and coffee in a casual, industrial-chic setting. Focusing on fresh, locally sourced ingredients, it is perfect for a light lunch or a quick pick-me-up.

Poppo's Taqueria ($)
1544 Main St, Sarasota, FL 34236,
Phone: (941) 706-2849   www.poppostaqueria.com/

This fast-casual Mexican eatery is known for its delicious tacos, burritos, and quesadillas made with fresh, locally sourced ingredients. Build your meal with various tasty fillings and toppings, and do not forget to try their homemade hot sauces.

Daily Eats ($$)
8491 Cooper Creek Blvd, Sarasota, FL 34201,
Phone: (941) 208-3887   www.dailyeatssarasota.com/

Daily Eats serves up creative comfort food in a modern, relaxed setting. With hearty breakfast options, fresh salads, and unique bowls, there is something for every taste and dietary preference.

IL Panificio ($$)
1703 Main St, Sarasota, FL 34236,
Phone: (941) 366-5570   www.ilpanificiousa.com/

This local Italian bakery and pizzeria serve delicious, made-to-order pizzas, sandwiches, and pastries. The laid-back atmosphere and delicious food make it an ideal spot for a quick and satisfying meal.

Veronica Fish & Oyster ($$$)
1830 S Osprey Ave, Sarasota, FL 34239,
Phone: (941) 366-1342
www.veronicafishandoyster.com/

This stylish seafood bar offers a selection of raw and cooked seafood dishes and various craft cocktails. The innovative menu and upscale atmosphere make it a must-visit for seafood lovers.

SARASOTA UNCOVERED

Toasted Mango Café ($$)
430 N Tamiami Trail, Sarasota, FL 34236,
Phone: (941) 388-7728
www.toastedmangocafe.com/

The Toasted Mango Café is a cheerful breakfast and lunch spot serving classic dishes with a twist. With a focus on fresh ingredients and friendly service, it is a perfect choice for a leisurely brunch or a quick bite.

Origin Craft Beer & Pizza Café ($$)
1837 Hillview St, Sarasota, FL 34239,
Phone: (941) 300-1043   www.originsrq.com/

Origin combines the best of both worlds – craft beer and artisan pizza. With a rotating selection of local and international brews and a menu of inventive, wood-fired pizzas, it is a popular choice for a laid-back meal with friends.

Gecko's Grill & Pub ($$)
4870 S Tamiami Trail, Sarasota, FL 34231,
Phone: (941) 923-8896   www.geckosgrill.com/

Gecko's is a local institution known for its friendly atmosphere, delicious pub fare, and extensive craft beer list. With live sports on TV and a menu of hearty burgers, sandwiches, and wings, it is an excellent spot for a casual meal and catching up with friends.

Chapter 27 /
Bars and Nightclubs

Sarasota, a sun-soaked gem on Florida's Gulf Coast, boasts a vibrant nightlife scene that caters to diverse tastes and preferences. From laid-back beach bars to swanky lounges, the city's hotspots promise an unforgettable night out, whether you are a local or just visiting. Here are the nightlife destinations in the area, each offering a unique atmosphere and plenty of reasons to raise your glass.

SARASOTA UNCOVERED

Siesta Key Oyster Bar ($$)
5238 Ocean Blvd, Sarasota, FL 34242.
(941) 346-5443   www.skob.com.

Known by locals as SKOB, this popular island-style hangout offers a laid-back atmosphere with live music, delicious seafood, and a wide selection of refreshing drinks. Located just steps from Siesta Key Beach, this is the perfect spot to unwind after a day in the sun.

O'Leary's Tiki Bar & Grill ($)
Bayfront Dr, Sarasota, FL 34236.
(941) 953-7505   www.olearystikibar.com

This lively waterfront tiki bar features a casual, tropical vibe with unbeatable views of Sarasota Bay. Enjoy live music, a delicious seafood menu, and various tropical drinks while watching the sunset.

Pangea Alchemy Lab ($$$)
1564 Main St, Sarasota, FL 34236.
(941) 870-5555   www.pangealounge.com

Step into this speakeasy-style cocktail bar for a sophisticated evening of creative libations and intimate conversation. Pangea's skilled mixologists craft unique and artfully presented cocktails in a cozy, dimly lit space.

Smokin' Joe's Pub ($$)
1448 Main St, Sarasota, FL 34236.
(941) 955-7761   www.smokinjoespub.com

A friendly neighborhood pub with a great selection of craft beer, pool tables, and a casual, welcoming atmosphere. Smokin' Joe's is the perfect spot to grab a pint, shoot some pool, and enjoy great conversation with locals.

The Starlite Room ($$$)
1001 Cocoanut Ave, Sarasota, FL 34236
(941) 702-5613   www.starlitesrq.com

Inspired by Hollywood's Golden Age, this swanky lounge offers an elegant setting for a night out. Enjoy expertly crafted cocktails, live entertainment, and a menu of small gourmet plates in a chic, retro ambiance.

The Beach Club ($$)
5151 Ocean Blvd, Sarasota, FL 34242
(941) 349-6311   www.beachclubsiestakey.com

Located on Siesta Key, The Beach Club is a lively hotspot offering a spacious dance floor, live DJs, and a full bar. With themed nights and a vibrant atmosphere, this is the place to let loose and dance the night away.

Libby's Neighborhood Brasserie ($$$)
1917 S Osprey Ave, Sarasota, FL 34239
(941) 487-7300
www.libbysneighborhoodbrasserie.com

A stylish, upscale brasserie that boasts an extensive wine list, a full bar, and a menu of delicious, contemporary cuisine. Its sophisticated setting is perfect for date night or a special occasion.

Mattison's City Grille ($$)
1 N Lemon Ave, Sarasota, FL 34236
(941) 330-0440
www.mattisons.com/mattisons-city-grille/

This open-air downtown eatery offers a lively atmosphere with live music, a diverse menu, and a full bar. It is an ideal spot for enjoying a delicious meal, drinks, and entertainment under the stars.

SARASOTA UNCOVERED

The Blue Rooster ($$)
1525 4th St, Sarasota, FL 34236
(941) 388-7539   www.blueroostersrq.com

If you are a fan of live music, especially blues and jazz, The Blue Rooster is a must-visit. This Southern-style bar and restaurant offer a fantastic lineup of local and touring musicians, mouthwatering comfort food, and a vibrant, welcoming atmosphere.

Cock & Bull ($$)
975 Cattlemen Rd, Sarasota, FL 34232
(941) 363-1262   www.the-cock-n-bull.com

A local favorite for beer enthusiasts, Cock & Bull boasts an impressive selection of craft brews, a dog-friendly beer garden, and a lively atmosphere. The venue regularly hosts live music, trivia nights, and other events, making it a great spot to meet new friends and enjoy a pint.

Mandeville Beer Garden ($$)
428 N Lemon Ave, Sarasota, FL 34236
(941) 954-8688   www.mandevillebeergarden.com

This unique, indoor-outdoor beer garden offers an extensive selection of craft beers, a delicious food menu, and plenty of games to keep you entertained, including cornhole, giant Jenga, and foosball. It is a fun, family-friendly spot to spend a relaxing evening.

The Reserve ($$$)
1322 N Tamiami Trl, Sarasota, FL 34236
(941) 702-5859   www.thereservesrq.com

This versatile venue serves as a coffee shop, wine bar, and bookstore, offering a cozy, sophisticated atmosphere perfect for a laid-back evening. Enjoy a glass of wine or a craft beer, live music, and an assortment of tasty small plates.

Bahi Hut Lounge ($$)
4675 N Tamiami Trl, Sarasota, FL 34234
(941) 355-5141   www.bahihut.com

A Sarasota institution since 1954, Bahi Hut Lounge is an iconic tiki bar serving potent tropical drinks in a kitschy, vintage-inspired atmosphere. Sip on a classic Mai Tai or Zombie and soak in the retro charm of this beloved local spot.

State Street Eating House + Cocktails ($$$)
1533 State St, Sarasota, FL 34236
(941) 951-1533   www.statestreetsrq.com

This stylish, modern gastropub offers an impressive selection of handcrafted cocktails, an eclectic menu of gourmet fare, and a sleek, contemporary ambiance. It is an excellent destination for a night out with friends or a romantic date.

SARASOTA UNCOVERED

Chapter 28 /
Wine and Liquor Stores

Sarasota, Florida, offers many wine and liquor venues for leisure and business travelers. Whether you are looking for a cozy wine bar, a lively brewery, or a well-stocked liquor store, this beautiful coastal city has something for everyone. Here, we present venues to satisfy your thirst for wine, liquor, beer, and cigars.

Michael's Wine Cellar
1283 S Tamiami Trail, Sarasota, FL 34239
Phone: (941) 955-2675   www.michaelswinecellar.com

Siesta Key Rum
2212 Industrial Blvd, Sarasota, FL 34234
Phone: (941) 702-8143   www.siestakeyrum.com

Total Wine & More
8539 S Tamiami Trail, Sarasota, FL 34238
Phone: (941) 925-0341   www.totalwine.com

The Reserve
1322 N Tamiami Trail, Sarasota, FL 34236
Phone: (941) 702-9933   www.thereservesrq.com

Sarasota Fine Wine & Tastings
3980 S Tamiami Trail, Sarasota, FL 34231
Phone: (941) 366-2277   www.sarasotafinewine.com

Louie's Modern
1289 N Palm Ave, Sarasota, FL 34236
Phone: (941) 552-9688   www.louiesmodern.com

Big Top Brewing Company
6111 Porter Way, Sarasota, FL 34232
Phone: (941) 371-2939   www.bigtopbrewing.com

Sarasota Wine Vault
1788 N Honore Ave, Sarasota, FL 34235
Phone: (941) 377-9463   www.sarasotawinevault.com

JDub's Brewing Company
1215 Mango Ave, Sarasota, FL 34237
Phone: (941) 955-2739   www.jdubsbrewing.com

Smokin' Joes
1448 Main St, Sarasota, FL 34236
Phone: (941) 955-6010   www.smokinjoespub.com

Corkscrew Deli
4982 S Tamiami Trail, Sarasota, FL 34231
Phone: (941) 925-3955   www.corkscrewdeli.com

SARASOTA UNCOVERED

Mandeville Beer Garden
428 N Lemon Ave, Sarasota, FL 34236
Phone: (941) 954-8688
www.mandevillebeergarden.com

Growler's Pub
2831 N Tamiami Trail, Sarasota, FL 34234
Phone: (941) 487-7373   www.growlerspub.com

Beneva Wines & Spirits
4466 S Beneva Rd, Sarasota, FL 34233
Phone: (941) 924-9400   www.benevawines.com

Libby's
1917 S Osprey Ave, Sarasota, FL 34239
Phone: (941) 487- 7300
www.libbysneighborhoodbrasserie.com

Calusa Brewing
5701 Derek Ave, Sarasota, FL 34238
Phone: (941) 922-8150   www.calusabrewing.com

99 Bottles
1445 2nd St, Sarasota, FL 34236
Phone: (941) 487-7874   www.99bottlessarasota.com

Brew Life Brewing
5767 Beneva Rd, Sarasota, FL 34233
Phone: (941) 952-3831   www.brewlifebrewing

Motorworks Brewing
1014 9th St W, Bradenton, FL 34205 (Just outside Sarasota)
Phone: (941) 567-6218 www.motorworksbrewing.com

Chapter 29 /.
CRAFT BREWERIES

Sarasota, Florida, is a haven for beautiful beaches, art, and culture and a thriving hotspot for craft beer fans. As the craft brewery movement continues gaining momentum nationwide, Sarasota has emerged as a critical player in the industry, boasting a diverse array of breweries, each with its unique approach to beer-making. In this picturesque Gulf Coast city, you will find an enticing blend of traditional brewing methods and innovative techniques that push the boundaries of flavor and creativity.

The bustling brewery scene in Sarasota offers something for everyone, from casual beer drinkers to the most discerning connoisseurs. With an emphasis on locally sourced ingredients and a passion for perfecting their craft, Sarasota's brewers consistently produce high-quality, delicious brews that can hold their own against some of the best beers in the world. From hoppy IPAs to rich,

SARASOTA UNCOVERED

velvety stouts, these breweries' array of flavors and styles is nothing short of impressive.

But it is not just the beer that makes Sarasota's craft brewery scene so unique—it is also the vibrant community that has grown around it. Many of these breweries serve as social hubs where friends can gather to catch up over a cold pint or where strangers can bond over a shared love of beer. Often featuring live music, food trucks, and special events, these breweries provide a welcoming atmosphere that fosters camaraderie and a sense of belonging.

In addition to the friendly, laid-back vibes, these breweries are committed to sustainability and giving back to the community. From using eco-friendly practices to supporting local farmers and charities, these establishments embody the spirit of social responsibility and demonstrate that brewing great beer can go hand in hand with positively impacting the world.

As you embark on your journey to explore Sarasota's flourishing craft brewery scene, you will not only be treated to some of the finest brews the Sunshine State has to offer but also can immerse yourself in a thriving, enthusiastic community that celebrates the art of beer-making. So, grab a pint, sit back, and prepare to experience the absolute best of Sarasota's craft breweries.

JDub's Brewing Company & Tap Room ($$)
1215 Mango Ave, Sarasota, FL 34237
Phone: (941) 955-2739   jdubsbrewing.com

JDub's is a local favorite known for its innovative brews and laid-back atmosphere. They offer various beers, from hoppy IPAs to crisp lagers, ensuring something for everyone.

Big Top Brewing Company ($$)
6111 Porter Way, Sarasota, FL 34232 Phone: (941) 371-2939   bigtopbrewing.com

Big Top Brewing Company pays homage to Sarasota's circus heritage with its circus-themed taproom and eclectic lineup of beers, ranging from bold stouts to refreshing fruit-infused ales.

Calusa Brewing ($$)
5701 Derek Ave, Sarasota, FL 34233 Phone: (941) 922-8150   calusabrewing.com

Calusa Brewing prides itself on its artfully crafted beers, focusing on hop-forward and barrel-aged offerings. Their spacious taproom and beer garden is perfect for a relaxing afternoon or evening.

Mandeville Beer Garden ($$)
428 N Lemon Ave, Sarasota, FL 34236
Phone: (941) 954-8688   mandevillebeergarden.com

Mandeville Beer Garden is a family-friendly spot offering a diverse selection of local and international craft beers and a tasty menu. The outdoor space features games, making it a great place to hang out with friends and family.

SARASOTA UNCOVERED

Motorworks Brewing ($$)
1014 9th St W, Bradenton, FL 34205
Phone: (941) 567-6218   motorworksbrewing.com

Located just outside Sarasota in Bradenton, Motorworks Brewing is a popular destination for craft beer enthusiasts. They offer an extensive lineup of beers, from crisp pilsners to rich porters, served in a lively taproom and beer garden.

Sarasota Brewing Company** ($$)
6607 Gateway Ave, Sarasota, FL 34231
Phone: (941) 925-2337   sarasotabrewing.com

Sarasota Brewing Company is a longstanding local institution featuring a range of house-made beers alongside mouthwatering pub fare. The welcoming atmosphere makes it an ideal spot for casual gatherings and beer tastings.

Oak & Stone ($$$)
4067 Clark Rd, Sarasota, FL 34233
Phone: (941) 893-4881   oakandstone.com

Oak & Stone is a unique craft beer destination that offers a self-serve beer wall, allowing guests to sample from over fifty taps. Pair your favorite brews with their artisanal wood-fired pizzas for a memorable experience.

Brew Life Brewing ($$)
5767 Beneva Rd, Sarasota, FL 34233
Phone: (941) 952-3831   brewlifebrewing.com

Brew Life Brewing is a small-batch brewery that focuses on creating unique, flavorful beers in a cozy, friendly environment. They offer a rotating selection of brews, ensuring there is always something new.

Keys Brewing & Eatery ($$)
2505 Manatee Ave E, Bradenton, FL 34208
Phone: (941) 218-0396 3keysbrewing.com

In nearby Bradenton, 3 Keys Brewing & Eatery is a family-owned brewery and restaurant offering diverse craft beers and delicious food. Their spacious patio and laid-back vibe make for a great outing with friends or family.

Good Liquid Brewing Company ($$)
4824 14th St W, Bradenton, FL 34207 Phone: (941) 896-6381 goodliquidbrewing.com

Good Liquid Brewing Company is another Bradenton gem featuring various beers on tap, including creative seasonal offerings. The brewery boasts a welcoming atmosphere, perfect for kicking back with a cold brew.

Chapter 30 /
A Spirited Journey

Picture this: you are cruising along the sun-soaked coastline of Sarasota, a warm breeze rustling through your hair, and you have one thing on your mind - the enticing world of distilleries. Florida may be known for its pristine beaches and thriving arts scene but tucked away within a few hours' drive are some of the finest distilleries you could ever visit. But, like a treasure trove waiting to be uncovered, these distilleries offer a taste of not just the local spirits but also the culture, history, and passion that make them truly one-of-a-kind.

So, buckle up and prepare to embark on a spirited journey, whether you are a whiskey connoisseur or a rum enthusiast. As you explore these distilleries, you will immerse yourself in their stories - stories woven with art, science, and magic. You will learn about the craft behind every sip, savor unique flavors, and forge memories that will linger long after the last drop.

To make your adventure more thrilling, we have compiled a list of the distilleries within a 2-hour drive of Sarasota, Florida. From the iconic to the hidden gems, these establishments boast a diverse range of spirits, experiences, and price points. Just follow the guide below and let the spirited journey begin!

Siesta Key Rum | $ |
2212 Industrial Blvd, Sarasota, FL 34234 |
(941) 702-8143 | siestakeyrum.com

Siesta Key Rum is a true Sarasota treasure. With award-winning handcrafted rums, this small-batch distillery is renowned for its exquisite flavors and warm, welcoming atmosphere. Visit for a tour and tasting to experience the passion behind every bottle.

Drum Circle Distilling | $$ |
6540 Superior Ave, Sarasota, FL 34231 |
(941) 926-7151 | drumcircledistilling.com

At Drum Circle Distilling, you will find small-batch spirits crafted with an emphasis on quality and sustainability. Their famous spiced rum has won accolades worldwide, making this eco-friendly distillery a must-visit for rum enthusiasts.

Cigar City Cider & Mead | $ |
1812 N 15th St, Tampa, FL 33605 |
(813) 242-6600 | cigarcitycider.com

Explore the world of cider and mead at Cigar City Cider & Mead. Located in Tampa's historic Ybor City, this laid-back venue offers an array of refreshing, handcrafted beverages made from Florida's finest fruits and honey.

SARASOTA UNCOVERED

St. Petersburg Distillery | $$$ |
800 31st St S, St. Petersburg, FL 33712 |
(727) 914-0931 | stpetedistillery.com

St. Petersburg Distillery takes you on a journey through time with its vintage-inspired craft spirits. Their artisanal gin, vodka, and whiskey are created using traditional methods and locally sourced ingredients, providing an authentic taste of Old Florida.

Dark Door Spirits | $$ |
6608 Anderson Rd, Tampa, FL 33634 |
(813) 531-4861 | darkdoorspirits.com
Unleash your adventurous side.

At Dark Door Spirits. This Tampa-based distillery is known for its innovative and daring approach to crafting spirits. With a lineup that includes unconventional gins and unique whiskey blends, a visit to Dark Door Spirits is a bold step into the unknown.

American Freedom Distillery | $$$ |
2232 5th Ave S, St. Petersburg, FL 33712 |
(727) 440-8337 | americanfreedomdistillery.com

American Freedom Distillery is steeped in history and patriotism. Founded by veterans, this St. Petersburg-based distillery offers a range of exceptional spirits, including their signature Horse Soldier Bourbon. Experience the taste of freedom and honor with every sip.

Loaded Cannon Distillery | $$ |
3115 Lakewood Ranch Blvd, Bradenton, FL 34211 |
(941) 900-1482   loadedcannondistillery.com

Loaded Cannon Distillery is the place to be for adventurous spirit enthusiasts. This Bradenton-based distillery boasts a creative range of handcrafted rums, vodkas, and whiskeys, perfect for those looking to explore new flavors and expand their palate.

Tampa Bay Rum Company | $ |
2102 E 4th Ave, Tampa, FL 33605 |
(813) 284-5485 | tampabayrumcompany.com

Tampa Bay Rum Company is a pirate's paradise. Located in Ybor City, this distillery offers a fun and lively atmosphere, complete with tastings of their Gasparilla Rum. Embrace your inner buccaneer and set sail for a swashbuckling adventure.

Florida Cane Distillery | $$ |
1820 N 15th St, Tampa, FL 33605 |
(813) 284-4975 | cane-vodka.com

Discover the essence of Florida at the Florida Cane Distillery. This Tampa-based distillery specializes in farm-to-bottle vodka, using only locally sourced ingredients. Enjoy a taste of the Sunshine State in every sip of their refreshing, fruit-infused creations.

Kozuba & Sons Distillery | $$$ |
1960 5th Ave S, St. Petersburg, FL 33712 |
(727) 201-9078 | kozubadistillery.com

Experience the fusion of old-world tradition and modern innovation at Kozuba & Sons Distillery. This family-owned establishment creates high-quality vodka, whiskey, and cordials, blending Polish techniques with Florida's abundant resources for a unique experience.

SARASOTA UNCOVERED

Chapter 31 /
Uncorking the Magic

A Wine Lover's Guide to Wineries Near Sarasota

Imagine this: you are basking in the warm Florida sun, the ocean breeze caressing your skin, and the air is filled with the sweet scent of grapes ripening on the vine. A veritable paradise for wine lovers, the area surrounding Sarasota is brimming with wineries that highlight the absolute best of Florida's terroir. Within a two-hour drive, you will find an enchanting world of wines waiting to be explored, each offering a unique blend of flavors, stories, and experiences.

As you embark on this voyage, you will discover that Florida's wineries are as diverse as the Sunshine State. From the rolling hills of rural estates to the charming coastal vineyards, there is something to suit every palate and preference. You will learn about the craft behind each glass, savor the taste of sun-kissed fruits, and create memories that will age as gracefully as a fine wine.

To help you navigate the abundant vineyards within a two-hour radius of Sarasota, we have curated a list of the wineries in the area. These venues cater to various tastes and budgets, featuring a mix of well-known names and hidden gems. Follow our guide and let the wine-tasting adventure begin!

Bunker Hill Vineyard & Winery | $$ |
8905 Bunker Hill Rd, Duette, FL 34219
(941) 776-0418   www.bunkerhillvineyard.com
Travel Time: 1 hour 15 minutes.

Nestled in the heart of Manatee County, Bunker Hill Vineyard & Winery prides itself on crafting eco-friendly, handcrafted wines. Visit this picturesque estate for a delightful tasting experience and learn about their sustainable winemaking practices.

Rosa Fiorelli Winery & Vineyard | $$ |
4250 County Rd 675, Bradenton, FL 34211
(941) 322-0976   www.fiorelliwinery.com
Travel Time: 50 minutes.

Rosa Fiorelli Winery & Vineyard is a family-owned gem producing award-winning wines in a warm and welcoming setting. Enjoy a guided tour and tasting at this charming Bradenton vineyard and savor the flavors of Florida's sun-kissed grapes.

SARASOTA UNCOVERED

Keel & Curley Winery | $ |
5210 W Thonotosassa Rd, Plant City, FL 33565
(813) 752-9100   www.keelandcurleywinery.com
Travel Time: 1 hour 30 minutes.

At Keel & Curley Winery, indulge in a unique fusion of wines and ciders. Located in Plant City, this innovative winery combines traditional winemaking with inventive techniques to create fruit-infused wines and refreshing ciders.

Murielle Winery | $$ |
13131 56th Ct, Clearwater, FL 33760
(727) 561-0336 | muriellewinery.com
Travel Time: 1 hour 15 minutes.

In Clearwater, Murielle Winery offers a diverse selection of handcrafted wines, from bold reds to crisp whites. Visit their elegant tasting room to sample their wide range of creations, including the famous Murielle Tropical Fruit Wine.

Aspirations Winery | $ |
22041 US Hwy 19 N, Clearwater, FL 33765
(727) 799-9463   www.aspirationswinery.com
Travel Time: 1 hour 20 minutes.**

Aspirations Winery is known for its small-batch, award-winning wines. Located in Clearwater, this boutique winery offers a cozy atmosphere for wine enthusiasts to sample their delightful creations, including fruit-infused blends and classic varietals.

Tarpon Springs Castle Winery | $$ |
320 E Tarpon Ave, Tarpon Springs, FL 34689
(727) 943-7029   www.tarponspringscastlewinery.com
Travel Time: 1 hour 30 minutes

Step into the enchanting world of Tarpon Springs Castle Winery, where Old World charm meets Florida's coastal beauty. Enjoy a personalized tasting experience in their elegant room, featuring a selection of handcrafted wines that capture the region's essence.

Lakeridge Winery & Vineyards | $$ |
19239 US-27, Clermont, FL 34715
| (800) 768-9463   www.lakeridgewinery.com
Travel Time: 2 hours.

Lakeridge Winery & Vineyards is a stunning estate set amid rolling hills in Clermont. With an extensive lineup of premium wines, this picturesque winery is a must-visit destination for those looking to immerse themselves in Florida's wine country.

Strong Tower Vineyard & Winery | $ |
17810 Forge Dr, Spring Hill, FL 34610
(352) 799-7612   www.strongtowervineyard.com
| Travel Time: 1 hour 45 minutes

Discover the natural beauty of Strong Tower Vineyard & Winery, a serene oasis in Spring Hill. Sample their estate-grown wines in the rustic tasting room and enjoy the stunning views of the lush vineyards surrounding you.

Two Lions Winery & Palm Harbor Brewery $$
1022 Georgia Ave, Palm Harbor, FL 34683
(727) 786-8039   twolionswinery.com
Travel Time: 1 hour 30 minutes.

Two Lions Winery & Palm Harbor Brewery offers the best of both worlds: exceptional wines and craft beers. Visit this eclectic venue in Palm Harbor for a unique tasting experience where you can explore various flavors and styles.

SARASOTA UNCOVERED

Chapter 32 / Places to Stay

Welcome to the sun-kissed shores of Sarasota, Florida, where the sparkling Gulf Coast meets unparalleled hospitality and relaxation. In this bustling beachside paradise, you will find a wide array of accommodations, each offering a unique blend of comfort, luxury, and charm. Sarasota has everything if you seek a serene sanctuary, a family-friendly resort, or a stylish boutique hotel. Immerse yourself in this coastal gem's warm and inviting atmosphere as you discover the perfect home away from home that caters to your every desire.

The Greater Sarasota area has hotels and resorts boasting world-class amenities, exceptional service, and awe-inspiring views. From opulent spa retreats to delightful beachfront bungalows, the range of accommodations ensures a perfect fit for every traveler. Imagine waking up to the gentle sound of waves lapping against the shore or enjoying a morning yoga session in a lush tropical garden. As the sun sets, indulge in gourmet cuisine or unwind with a refreshing cocktail by the pool. The possibilities are endless in this vibrant and enchanting destination.

The Ritz-Carlton, Sarasota $$$$$
1111 Ritz Carlton Dr, Sarasota, FL 34236
(941) 309-2000
www.ritzcarlton.com/en/hotels/florida/sarasota

This 5-star luxurious hotel offers upscale accommodations, a full-service spa, multiple dining options, and access to a private beach club on Lido Key. The elegant rooms and suites come with premium bedding, marble bathrooms, and stunning views of Sarasota Bay or the city skyline. Guests can also enjoy a Jack Nicklaus-designed golf course and a tennis center.

The Sarasota Modern $$$$
1290 Boulevard of the Arts, Sarasota, FL 34236
(941) 906-1290
www.thesarasotamodern.com/

A boutique hotel that seamlessly blends mid-century modern design with urban sophistication, The Sarasota Modern features spacious rooms and suites, a rooftop pool, and on-site dining. Guests can enjoy various amenities, including a fitness center, poolside cabanas, and access to nearby downtown attractions.

SARASOTA UNCOVERED

Lido Beach Resort $$$$
700 Benjamin Franklin Dr, Sarasota, FL 34236
(941) 388-2161
www.lidobeachresort.com/

Located on Lido Key, this beachfront resort boasts various accommodations, from standard guest rooms to spacious suites with full kitchens. Guests can take advantage of the resort's two heated pools, a beachside Tiki bar, and on-site dining with breathtaking Gulf views. Water sports rentals and beach services are also available.

Hyatt Regency Sarasota $$$$
1000 Boulevard of the Arts, Sarasota, FL 34236
(941) 953-1234
www.hyatt.com/en-US/hotel/florida/hyatt-regency-sarasota/srqss

This downtown waterfront hotel offers modern rooms, a private marina, an outdoor pool, on-site dining, and convenient access to nearby attractions like the Van Wezel Performing Arts Hall and the Sarasota Opera House. The hotel also features 20,000 square feet of versatile event space, making it an ideal destination for meetings and extraordinary events.

Art Ovation Hotel $$$$
1255 N Palm Ave, Sarasota, FL 34236
(941) 316-0808
www.artovationhotel.com/

Located in the heart of downtown Sarasota, this art-themed boutique hotel offers uniquely designed rooms, a rooftop pool and bar, on-site dining, and various cultural experiences, including artist talks, live performances, and art classes. In addition, guests can also explore the nearby theaters, galleries, and restaurants that make Sarasota's art scene vibrant.

Carlisle Inn Sarasota $$$
3727 Bahia Vista St, Sarasota, FL 34232
(844) 369-2275
www.dhgroup.com/inns/carlisle-inn-sarasota/

Inspired by Amish artistry and hospitality, this hotel features comfortable rooms with handcrafted furnishings, an outdoor pool, a fitness center, and a complimentary breakfast. The Carlisle Inn is located near Pinecraft Park, providing guests with a unique and peaceful retreat in the heart of Sarasota.

Hotel Indigo Sarasota $$$
1223 Boulevard of the Arts, Sarasota, FL 34236
(941) 487-3800
www.ihg.com/hotelindigo/hotels/us/en/sarasota/srqsd/hoteldetail

This stylish hotel in the Rosemary District offers modern rooms, a rooftop pool, and on-site dining at the H2O Bistro. Guests can easily access downtown attractions, including the Sarasota Opera House, Van Wezel Performing Arts Hall, and The Ringling Museum. The hotel's vibrant design and attentive staff create a memorable stay.

Aloft Sarasota $$$
1401 Ringling Blvd, Sarasota, FL 34236
(941) 870-0900
www.marriott.com/hotels/travel/srqal-aloft-sarasota/

This trendy hotel features contemporary rooms with colorful, modern decor, a rooftop pool and lounge, an on-site bar, and live music. Located in downtown Sarasota, the hotel is within walking distance of popular attractions, including the Sarasota Opera House, the Florida Studio Theatre, and Marina Jack.

SARASOTA UNCOVERED

Embassy Suites by Hilton Sarasota $$$$
202 N Tamiami Trail, Sarasota, FL 34236
(941) 256-0190
www.hilton.com/en/hotels/srqeses-embassy-suites-sarasota/

This all-suite hotel in downtown Sarasota offers spacious rooms with separate living areas, fully equipped kitchens, and private balconies. Guests can enjoy a complimentary cooked-to-order breakfast, evening reception, outdoor pool, and on-site dining at Bridges Restaurant. The hotel is within walking distance of attractions like the Van Wezel Performing Arts Hall and the Sarasota Art Museum.

Westin Sarasota $$$$
100 Marina View Dr, Sarasota, FL 34236
(941) 217-4777
www.marriott.com/hotels/travel/srqwi-the-Westin-sarasota/

This upscale hotel offers luxurious rooms with stunning views, a rooftop pool and bar, a full-service spa, a fitness center, and multiple on-site dining options. Located in downtown Sarasota, the hotel is close to attractions such as the Marie Selby Botanical Gardens, The Ringling Museum, and St. Armands Circle.

Siesta Key Beach Resort & Suites $$
5311 Ocean Blvd, Sarasota, FL 34242
(941) 349-1236
www.siestakeybeachresortandsuites.com/

This casual resort offers cozy rooms, suites, and villas steps from the award-winning Siesta Key Beach. Guests can enjoy a heated pool, outdoor seating, and complimentary beach equipment rentals. The resort is also within walking distance of Siesta Key Village, which offers various shops, restaurants, and entertainment options.

The Resort at Longboat Key Club $$$$
220 Sands Point Rd, Longboat Key, FL 34228
(941) 383-8821
www.longboatkeyclub.com/

This beachfront resort offers upscale accommodations, a 45-hole golf course, 20 Har-Tru tennis courts, a full-service spa, multiple dining options, and a 291-slip marina. With a range of recreational activities and luxurious amenities, the resort provides an idyllic getaway on Longboat Key.

Sandcastle Resort at Lido Beach $$$
1540 Ben Franklin Dr, Sarasota, FL 34236
(941) 388-2181
www.sandcastlelidobeach.com/

This beachfront resort features comfortable rooms, suites, villas, two heated pools, a beachside Tiki bar, and on-site dining. Located on Lido Key, the resort is just a short drive from St. Armands Circle, offering shopping, dining, and entertainment. Guests can also enjoy complimentary beach chairs and umbrellas.

The Sarasota Bay Club $$$$
301 N Tamiami Trail, Sarasota, FL 34236
(941) 366-7667
www.sarasotabayclub.net/

This luxury retirement community offers independent living, assisted living, and skilled nursing services. Residents can enjoy beautiful waterfront views, elegant apartments, various amenities, and a full calendar of social and cultural activities. Located on the shores of Sarasota Bay, the community is close to downtown attractions, including the Van Wezel Performing Arts Hall and the Sarasota Opera House.

SARASOTA UNCOVERED

Turtle Beach Resort & Inn $$$
9049 Midnight Pass Rd, Sarasota, FL 34242
(941) 349-4554
www.turtlebeachresort.com/

This quaint resort offers charming cottages and suites on Siesta Key, just steps from the beach. Guests can enjoy private hot tubs, fully equipped kitchens, and waterfront views. The resort also provides complimentary use of kayaks, canoes, and bicycles for exploring the beautiful surroundings.

Homewood Suites Sarasota-Lakewood Ranch $$$
305 N Cattlemen Rd, Sarasota, FL 34243,
(941) 365-7300
www.hilton.com/en/hotels/srqhwhw-homewood-suites-sarasota-lakewood-ranch/

This all-suite hotel offers spacious rooms with full kitchens, separate living areas, and complimentary Wi-Fi. Guests can enjoy a daily hot breakfast, an evening social reception, an outdoor pool, and a fitness center. The hotel is near attractions such as the Mall at University Town Center and Nathan Benderson Park.

Hampton Inn & Suites Sarasota/Bradenton Airport $$
975 University Pkwy, Sarasota, FL 34243
Phone (941) 355-8140
www.hilton.com/en/hotels/srqaphx-Hampton-suites-sarasota-bradenton-airport/

This comfortable hotel offers modern rooms, complimentary breakfast, and an outdoor pool, all close to Sarasota-Bradenton International Airport and the Ringling Museum. Guests can also take advantage of the hotel's fitness center and 24-hour business center.

Holiday Inn Lido Beach $$$
233 Ben Franklin Dr, Sarasota, FL 34236
(941) 388-5555
www.ihg.com/holidayinn/hotels/us/en/sarasota/srqlb/hoteldetail

This beachfront hotel features comfortable rooms with private balconies, a rooftop pool offering stunning views, and on-site dining at the Sand Dollar Rooftop Restaurant. Guests can easily access Lido Beach and the shops and restaurants at St. Armands Circle.

Courtyard by Marriott Sarasota University Park / Lakewood Ranch Area $$$
8305 Tourist Center Dr, Sarasota, FL 34201,
(941) 360-2626
www.marriott.com/hotels/travel/srqcy-courtyard-sarasota-university-park-lakewood-ranch-area/

This contemporary hotel offers comfortable rooms and suites, an outdoor pool, a fitness center, and on-site dining at The Bistro. Located near the Mall at University Town Center, the hotel provides easy access to shopping, dining, entertainment options, and the beautiful beaches of Sarasota.

Sleep Inn/Mainstay Suites Sarasota I-75 $$
5965 Brookhill Blvd, Sarasota, FL 34232,
(941) 500-4700
www.choicehotels.com/florida/sarasota/sleep-inn-hotels/flj63

This dual-concept hotel offers traditional guest rooms and extended-stay suites, featuring fully equipped kitchens and separate living areas. In addition, guests can enjoy a complimentary breakfast, an outdoor pool, a fitness center, and laundry facilities. The hotel is near attractions such as the Mall at University Town Center, Nathan Benderson Park, and the Sarasota Polo Club.

SARASOTA UNCOVERED

Chapter 33 / Camping

Imagine waking up to the sound of birdsong, the smell of the great outdoors, and the gentle sway of trees above your head. Camping is a fantastic way to disconnect from the hustle and bustle of everyday life and reconnect with nature, friends, and family. And there is no better place to pitch your tent or park your RV than in the beautiful surroundings of Sarasota, Florida. Sarasota is a camper's paradise with its warm climate, diverse ecosystems, and stunning Gulf Coast scenery. Whether seeking a peaceful retreat or an adventure-filled getaway, you will find a wealth of campgrounds and RV parks that cater to all tastes, budgets, and preferences.

Sarasota's campgrounds offer many facilities and experiences, from beachside locations with mesmerizing sunsets to lush forest hideaways. You will find well-

maintained sites with full hookups for RVs, primitive spots for tent camping, and everything in between. Plus, with many of these campgrounds near popular attractions, you will never run out of activities to enjoy. Instead, hike through verdant nature trails, swim in clear waters, or relax by a crackling campfire under a starry night sky. In Sarasota, the possibilities are endless.

So, grab your camping gear, load up your RV or pack your tent, and embark on a journey of exploration and relaxation in the great outdoors of Sarasota, Florida. To help you plan your camping adventure, we have compiled a list of the area's campgrounds and RV parks, complete with descriptions, addresses, contact information, and a handy price guide.

Turtle Beach Campground
RVs with hookups, Electric service, Water, and sewer
8862 Midnight Pass Rd, Sarasota, FL 34242
Phone: (941) 349-3839
www.turtlebeachcampground.com

Nestled on Siesta Key's southern tip, Turtle Beach Campground is a beach lover's dream. This beautiful campground offers 39 RV sites with full hookups, electric service, water, and sewer. Guests can enjoy easy access to the sandy shores, fishing, boating, and a playground for the kids.

SARASOTA UNCOVERED

Myakka River State Park
RVs and tent camping, Electric Service, Water
13208 State Rd 72, Sarasota, FL 34241
Phone: (941) 361-6511
www.floridastateparks.org/parks-and-trails/myakka-river-state-park

Experience Florida's wild side at Myakka River State Park, one of the state's oldest and largest parks. With 76 RV and tent campsites featuring electric service and water, you will have a comfortable base to explore the park's diverse habitats, hiking trails, and abundant wildlife.

Sarasota Bay RV Park
RVs with hookups, Electric service, Water, and sewer
10777 Cortez Rd W, Bradenton, FL 34210
Phone: (941) 794-1200
www.sarasotabayrvpark.com

Sarasota Bay RV Park is a waterfront oasis perfect for those seeking a more luxurious camping experience. This 55+ RV park features 246 sites with full hookups, electric service, water, and sewer. Enjoy the heated pool, clubhouse, and stunning views of Sarasota Bay.

Sun-N-Fun RV Resort**
RVs with hookups, Electric service, Water, and sewer
7125 Fruitville Rd, Sarasota, FL 34240
Phone: (941) 371-2505
www.carefreervresorts.com/sun-n-fun

Sun-N-Fun RV Resort is a premier destination for relaxation and recreation. With over 600 RV sites featuring full hookups, electric service, water, and sewer, you will find everything you need for a comfortable stay. Enjoy amenities like a heated pool, fitness center, and various activities and events.

Oscar Scherer State Park
RVs and tent camping, Electric Service, Water
1843 S Tamiami Trail, Osprey, FL 34229
Phone: (941) 483-5956
www.floridastateparks.org/parks-and-trails/oscar-scherer-state-park

Oscar Scherer State Park offers a serene camping experience amidst diverse habitats and wildlife. You will have a peaceful retreat close to nature with 104 RV and tent campsites featuring electric service and water. Explore the park's hiking trails, kayak on the waterways, or enjoy a refreshing swim.

Lake Manatee State Park
RVs and tent camping, Electric Service, Water
20007 E State Rd 64, Bradenton, FL 34212
Phone: (941) 741-3028
www.floridastateparks.org/parks-and-trails/lake-manatee-state-park

Lake Manatee State Park is a haven for nature lovers and water enthusiasts. The park offers 60 RV and tent campsites with electric service and water. Enjoy fishing, boating, and swimming in the 2,400-acre lake, or explore the park's scenic nature trails.

Ramblers Rest RV Resort
RVs with hookups, Electric service, Water, and sewer
1300 N River Rd, Venice, FL 34293
Phone: (941) 493-4354
www.ramblersrestrvresort.com

Nestled along the Myakka River, Ramblers Rest RV Resort is a picturesque location for a tranquil camping getaway. This 55+ resort offers 400 RV sites with full hookups, electric service, water, and sewer. Amenities include a heated pool, fitness center, and various activities and clubs.

SARASOTA UNCOVERED

Creekside RV Resort
RVs with hookups, Electric service, Water, and sewer
27005 Jones Loop Rd, Punta Gorda, FL 33982
Phone: (941) 833-3334   www.creeksidervresort.com

For a luxurious RV camping experience, head to Creekside RV Resort. This upscale resort features 162 RV sites with full hookups, electric service, water, and sewer. Enjoy the heated pool, fitness center, and clubhouse, or participate in the many planned activities and events.

Little Manatee River State Park
RVs and tent camping, Electric Service, Water
215 Lightfoot Rd, Wima
Phone: (813) 671-5005
www.floridastateparks.org/parks-and-trails/little-manatee-river-state-park

Discover the beauty of Little Manatee River State Park, a serene natural oasis with diverse ecosystems. The park offers 34 RV and tent campsites with electric service and water. Explore the park's hiking trails, kayak or canoe on the river, or unwind and enjoy the tranquil surroundings.

Winter Quarters Manatee RV Resort
RVs with hookups, Electric service, Water, and sewer
800 Kay Rd NE, Bradenton, FL 34212
Phone: (941) 745-2500
www.rvonthego.com/florida/winter-quarters-manatee-rv

Experience a warm and welcoming atmosphere at Winter Quarters Manatee RV Resort. This 55+ resort features 340 RV sites with full hookups, electric service, water, and sewer. Enjoy the heated pool, shuffleboard courts, and various activities and events to keep you entertained throughout your stay.

Chapter 34 /
Airport Transportation

Traveling to Sarasota, Florida, is an adventure that starts the moment you step off the plane. Imagine the sun-kissed beaches, clear waters, and vibrant arts scene waiting for you to explore. But to embark on this journey, you will need a reliable and comfortable way to get from the airport to your chosen destination. That is where airport transportation comes into play. In this Chapter, we will guide you through Sarasota's top airport transportation options, ensuring your trip begins smoothly and hassle-free.

SARASOTA UNCOVERED

Sarasota Airport Shuttle Price: $$
www.sarasotaairportshuttle.com

Airports Served: Sarasota-Bradenton International Airport (SRQ) Sarasota Airport Shuttle offers reliable and punctual shuttle services from Sarasota-Bradenton International Airport. Their comfortable vans and professional drivers will easily ensure you reach your destination.

Suncoast Limousine Services Price: $$$
www.suncoastlimo.com

Airports Served: Sarasota-Bradenton International Airport (SRQ), Tampa International Airport (TPA), St. Petersburg-Clearwater International Airport (PIE) For a touch of luxury, Suncoast Limousine Services offers stylish transportation to and from the airport. Their fleet of high-end vehicles, including sedans and SUVs, promises a comfortable and sophisticated ride.

Blue Dolphin Shuttle Price: $
www.bluedolphinshuttle.com

Airports Served: Sarasota-Bradenton International Airport (SRQ) Blue Dolphin Shuttle is an affordable and dependable option for airport transfers in Sarasota. With their friendly drivers and timely service, you will enjoy a stress-free start to your vacation.

Siesta Key Airport Taxi Price: $$
www.siestakeyairporttaxi.com

Airports Served: Sarasota-Bradenton International Airport (SRQ), Tampa International Airport (TPA) Siesta Key Airport Taxi specializes in transportation between the airport and the idyllic barrier islands of Sarasota. Their knowledgeable drivers ensure a smooth and enjoyable ride.

Elegant Airport Shuttle Price: $$$
www.elegantairportshuttle.com

Airports Served: Sarasota-Bradenton International Airport (SRQ), Tampa International Airport (TPA), St. Petersburg-Clearwater International Airport (PIE)
Elegant Airport Shuttle offers luxury transportation services for travelers seeking a refined experience. Their fleet includes well-maintained sedans and SUVs, guaranteeing a comfortable journey.

Sarasota Taxi Company Price: $
www.sarasotataxicompany.com

Airports Served: Sarasota-Bradenton International Airport (SRQ)
Sarasota Taxi Company is a budget-friendly option for airport transfers, providing traditional taxi services. Their experienced drivers and well-maintained vehicles ensure a pleasant ride to your destination.

Sarasota Luxury Car Service Price: $$$
www.sarasotaluxurycarservice.com

Airports Served: Sarasota-Bradenton International Airport (SRQ), Tampa International Airport (TPA), St. Petersburg-Clearwater International Airport (PIE)
For a high-end airport transportation experience, Sarasota Luxury Car Service offers a range of premium vehicles to cater to your needs. Their professional chauffeurs will ensure a seamless journey.

SARASOTA UNCOVERED

Shoreline Airport Shuttle Price: $$
www.shorelineairportshuttle.com

Airports Served: Sarasota-Bradenton International Airport (SRQ), Tampa International Airport (TPA)
Shoreline Airport Shuttle is a trusted choice for airport transportation, providing prompt service and friendly drivers. Their well-maintained vehicles will ensure a comfortable ride to your destination.

Sarasota Airport Express Price: $
www.sarasotaairportexpress.com

Airports Served: Sarasota-Bradenton International Airport (SRQ)
Sarasota Airport Express offers affordable shuttle services for travelers seeking a cost-effective option. In addition, their clean and comfortable vehicles guarantee a hassle-free transfer to your destination.

First Class Airport Transportation Price: $$$
www.firstclassairporttransportation.com

Airports Served: Sarasota-Bradenton International Airport (SRQ), Tampa International Airport (TPA), St. Petersburg-Clearwater International Airport (PIE)
First Class Airport Transportation provides luxury airport transfers for discerning travelers. Their selection of high-quality vehicles and professional chauffeurs promise an unparalleled transportation experience.

Chapter 35 / Weather

The following is a summary of the average weather conditions in Sarasota, Florida, including the number of sunny days, and rainy days, the average rainfall, and the monthly low and high temperatures:

January:
Sunny days: 17, Rainy days: 7, Average rainfall: 2.4 inches
Average low temperature: 52°F (11°C), Average high temperature: 71°F (22°C)

February:
Sunny days: 18, Rainy days: 6, Average rainfall: 2.6 inches
Average low temperature: 54°F (12°C), Average high temperature: 74°F (23°C)

March:
Sunny days: 22, Rainy days: 6, Average rainfall: 3.3 inches
Average low temperature: 58°F (14°C), Average high temperature: 77°F (25°C)

April:
Sunny days: 23, Rainy days: 5, Average rainfall: 2.2 inches
Average low temperature: 62°F (17°C), Average high temperature: 81°F (27°C)

May:
Sunny days: 25, Rainy days: 8, Average rainfall: 2.7 inches
Average low temperature: 68°F (20°C), Average high temperature: 87°F (31°C)

June:
Sunny days: 22, Rainy days: 14, Average rainfall: 8.2 inches
Average low temperature: 73°F (23°C), Average high temperature: 89°F (32°C)

SARASOTA UNCOVERED

July:

Sunny days: 22, Rainy days: 15, Average rainfall: 9.2 inches
Average low temperature: 74°F (23°C), Average high temperature: 90°F (32°C)

August:

Sunny days: 22, Rainy days: 16, Average rainfall: 9.7 inches
Average low temperature: 74°F (23°C), Average high temperature: 90°F (32°C)

September:

Sunny days: 21, Rainy days: 15, Average rainfall: 7.4 inches
Average low temperature: 73°F (23°C), Average high temperature: 89°F (32°C)

October:

Sunny days: 23, Rainy days: 7, Average rainfall: 3.1 inches
Average low temperature: 66°F (19°C), Average high temperature: 84°F (29°C)

November:

Sunny days: 20, Rainy days: 6, Average rainfall: 2.2 inches
Average low temperature: 59°F (15°C), Average high temperature: 78°F (26°C)

December:

Sunny days: 19, Rainy days: 8, Average rainfall: 2.6 inches
Average low temperature: 54°F (12°C), Average high temperature: 73°F (23°C)

Please note that these values are approximate averages and can vary from year to year. Therefore, checking the local weather forecast before your trip for the most up-to-date information is always a good idea.

: Chapter 36 /
Traveler Resource

1. Visit Sarasota (https://www.visitsarasota.com/): The official tourism website for Sarasota County, featuring information on accommodations, attractions, dining, events, and more.
2. Sarasota Chamber of Commerce (https://www.sarasotachamber.com/): Business directory, events calendar, visitor resources, and relocation information.
3. Siesta Key Chamber of Commerce (https://www.siestakeychamber.com/): Information on Siesta Key's businesses, accommodations, attractions, and a calendar of events.
4. Downtown Sarasota Alliance (https://www.downtownsarasota.com/): Information on downtown Sarasota's shops, restaurants, events, and attractions.
5. Sarasota County Area Transit (https://www.scgov.net/government/scat-bus-service): Details on public transportation options, including bus schedules and fares.
6. Sarasota-Bradenton International Airport (https://www.srq-airport.com/): Flight information, airport services, and transportation options for Sarasota and Bradenton.
7. Sarasota Bay Estuary Program (https://sarasotabay.org/): Information on Sarasota Bay's conservation efforts, recreational activities, and educational resources.
8. Sarasota County Parks, Recreation & Natural Resources (https://www.scgov.net/government/parks-recreation-and-natural-resources): Details on parks, beaches, and recreational facilities in Sarasota County.
9. Visit Florida (https://www.visitflorida.com/): The official tourism website for Florida, with comprehensive information on attractions, accommodations, and events throughout the state.

SARASOTA UNCOVERED

10. Florida State Parks (https://www.floridastateparks.org/): Information on state parks in Sarasota and throughout Florida, including fees, activities, and camping options.
11. Sarasota County Visitor Information Center (https://www.visitsarasota.com/visitor-information-center): Details on visitor services, including maps, brochures, and local information.
12. Sarasota County Libraries (https://www.scgov.net/government/libraries): Locations and services of public libraries in Sarasota County can be helpful for travelers.
13. Sarasota County Beaches (https://www.scgov.net/government/parks-recreation-and-natural-resources/find-a-park/beaches): Information on public beaches in Sarasota County, including amenities, parking, and facilities.
14. Sarasota County Bicycle/Pedestrian Trails (https://www.scgov.net/government/parks-recreation-and-natural-resources/find-a-park/trails): Information on walking, biking, and multi-use trails in Sarasota County.
15. Sarasota County Trolley Services (https://www.siestakeychamber.com/siesta-key-trolley/): Details on the free Siesta Key Breeze Trolley, offering transportation around Siesta Key.
16. Sarasota County Historical Resources (https://www.scgov.net/government/historical-resources): Information on historic sites and resources in Sarasota County, including museums and landmarks.
17. The City of Sarasota Parking (https://www.sarasotafl.gov/government/parking): Information on parking options and regulations within Sarasota.
18. Sarasota County Emergency Management (https://www.scgov.net/government/emergency-services/emergency-management):

Chapter 37 /
Emergency Numbers Hospitals and Walk-In Clinics

Always call 911 for immediate assistance or seek medical treatment in an emergency. The information provided below is intended for reference purposes only and should not be relied upon as the sole source of help during an emergency.

Emergency contact numbers for Sarasota,

Police: Sarasota Police Department -
(941) 263-6773 (non-emergency)
Fire: Sarasota County Fire Department
(941) 861-5000 (non-emergency)
Medical: Sarasota County Emergency Services
(941) 861-5000 (non-emergency)

Emergency Rooms in Sarasota,

Sarasota Memorial Hospital
1700 S Tamiami Trail, Sarasota, FL 34239
(941) 917-9000   WWW.Smh.com

Doctors Hospital of Sarasota - Emergency Room
5731 Bee Ridge Rd, Sarasota, FL 34233
(941) 342-1100   WWW.doctorsofsarasota.com

SARASOTA UNCOVERED

Walk-in Clinics in Sarasota, Florida:

Disclaimer: Neither the author nor the publisher has any affiliation, sponsorship, endorsement, or relationship with any urgent care providers listed in this publication. The information provided is for general reference purposes only. Therefore, we encourage you to research and exercise due diligence when selecting an urgent care facility to ensure it meets your needs and requirements.

Remember: in case of an emergency, always call 911 for immediate assistance or seek medical treatment. The information provided above is for reference purposes only and should not be relied upon as the sole source of help during an emergency.

Sarasota Urgent Care

6272 Lake Osprey Dr, Sarasota, FL 34240, (941) 907-2800
www.Sarasotaurgentcare.net, *Not open 24 hours

Concentra Urgent Care

1630 S. Tuttle Ave, Sarasota, FL 34239, (941) 906-2700
www.Concentra.com, *Not open 24 hours

MD Now Urgent Care

4071 Bee Ridge Rd, Sarasota, FL 34233, (941) 379-1800
www.mdnow.com, *Not open 24 hours

AFC Urgent Care Sarasota

2901 S Tamiami Trail, Sarasota, FL 34239, (941) 413-2888
www.afcurgentcaresarasota.com, *Not open 24 hours

CVS MinuteClinic

8330 S Tamiami Trail, Sarasota, FL 34238, (941) 927-3876
www.minuteclinic.com, *Not open 24 hours

Gulf Gate Medical Center

2075 Siesta Dr, Sarasota, FL 34239, (941) 923-5861
www.gulfgatemedical.com, *Not open 24 hours

MedExpress Urgent Care
3580 Bee Ridge Rd, Sarasota, FL 34233, (941) 379-6900
www.medexpress.com, *Not open 24 hours

Premier Medical Center
3595 Webber St, Sarasota, FL 34239, (941) 925-1900
www.premiermedicalcenter.com, *Not open 24 hours

Sarasota Walk-In Clinic
6272 Lake Osprey Dr, Sarasota, FL 34240, (941) 907-2800
www.sarasotawalkinclinic.net, *Not open 24 hours

StatMed Clinic
1801 Arlington St, Sarasota, FL 34239, (941) 366-7911
www.statmedclinic.com' *Not open 24 hours

SwiftCare Urgent Care
2455 Bee Ridge Rd, Sarasota, FL 34239, (941) 260-0045
www.swiftcareuc.com, *Not open 24 hours

Urgent Care Extra
5045 Fruitville Rd, Sarasota, FL 34232, (941) 342-1002
*Not open 24 hours

West Coast Urgent Care
3300 S Tamiami Trail, Sarasota, FL 34239, (941)366-9000
www.westcoasturgentcare.com, *Not open 24 hours

Bradenton Urgent Care
4647 Manatee Ave W, Bradenton, FL 34209, (941) 745-5999
www.bradentonurgentcare.com, *Not open 24 hours

Doctors Express Urgent Care
2901 University Pkwy Suite 100, Sarasota, FL 34243, (941) 358-0650,
www.doctorsexpresssarasota.com, *Not open 24 hours

SARASOTA UNCOVERED

ABOUT THE AUTHOR

Mike Avey is an adventurous spirit whose passion for travel and exploration is deeply rooted in his experiences growing up as a military kid. Mike's extraordinary life journey has taken him from working on an iron ore ship to studying in Boston, perfecting the art of woodworking, and serving as an emergency medic and firefighter. Eventually, he dove into the hospitality industry while exploring new cities and regions with the zeal of a local. His secret recipe for uncovering hidden gems and offbeat experiences. Adopting the mindset of a local wherever he goes!

With a dash of humor and a pinch of wanderlust, Mike has traversed the United States, the Caribbean, Central America, and Europe, employing every mode of transport imaginable. He's tried them all: planes, trains, automobiles, boats, ships, RVs, bicycles, or even electric bikes. Yet, his favorite exploration method remains strolling through the streets, soaking in the local atmosphere, and sparking impromptu conversations with passersby. By forging connections and asking the right questions, Mike has unearthed the best-kept secrets of each destination.

If Mike's adventures inspire you and approach travel, he welcomes you to reach out to him at
Mike@wordwavepublishing.com.

You can join his newsletter for the latest updates and travel tips by subscribing to
News@wordwavepublishing.com.
Embark on your journey with Mike Avey as your guide and uncover the hidden gems that await in every corner of the world.

MIKE AVEY

Made in the USA
Monee, IL
11 April 2024